OWN IT!

A GIRL'S GUIDE
TO BUILDING WEALTH

Margaret Wright

Editorial Project Management: Karen Rowe, KarenRowe.com

Cover Design: Daliborka Mijailović, dmijailovic73@gmail.com

Inside Layout: Mark Coleman, mark@markcolemandesign.com

Printed in the United States

ISBN: 978-0-9987804-0-5 (international trade paper edition)

ISBN: 978-0-9987804-1-2 (ebook)

This book is dedicated to all the women who are ready to make decisions based on what they would LOVE to do, rather than what they have to do based on what is in their bank account.

*"You either walk inside your story and own it
or you stand outside your story
and hustle for your worthiness."*
– Brené Brown

ADVANCE PRAISE FOR *OWN IT!*
A Girl's Guide to Building Wealth

If you have ever even considered investing in real estate, stop looking! With the knowledge and experience Margaret Wright has and is going to give you, you have no more excuses. In my first year flipping, I made over $63,000 in profits! No one else can put you in the driver seat faster!

—Annette Siwy
President, SARAF LLC

Margaret speaks to the heart of why women often fail to achieve the success and freedom they want from their lives… and most often it's because of our mindset! She provides deep insight into the challenges we face, and proposes practical yet achievable solutions you can benefit from immediately and every time you flip a house. She helps you cut the crap and just do it!

—GeNienne Samuels
President/CEO, GS Consulting & Communications

Through this book, Margaret Wright offers a valuable gift any woman who desires to have control of her world – not only through gaining financial independence, but through learning to adjust her beliefs and choices so that she can experience wealth in all areas of life. I will never flip another house without this book in my back pocket!

—Andrea Preston
Real Estate Investor, fellow flipper

If anything is holding you back from taking the first step in investing in real estate, you must pick up this book! Margaret Wright is a powerhouse in business and offers up some of the best strategies I have personally used to build passive income and generational wealth.

—*April Welsh*
full-time working mom of four

Margaret Wright offers the knowledge and strength for women looking to take control of their lives by achieving financial freedom and wealth on their own terms. She proves that having the right mindset is part of the process of a successful life.

—*Aimee Ensign*
CEO, A Gluten Free Me

A must-read for anyone who wants to flip a house, is scared to start or has been stuck in the process. Margaret shares her secrets for optimum wealth and freedom, in this engaging and inspiring treasure trove of information and experienced guidance!

—*Janet More*
Chief Geek Whisperer, The Geek Appeal Academy

Finally! A book that is completely missing the tired rhetoric and testosterone that fills most "how to" guides on real estate investing. Margaret Wright offers a fresh approach to building personal wealth and achieving financial freedom. One based on an inspired concept that women can and should take advantage of their unique abilities to be succeed in this male dominated field. Offering sound advice based on basic principles, this book is a must read for any woman wanting to take control of her own financial destiny and be wildly successful.

—*Melanie Carney*
Realtor and Investor

This is a very inspirational book for women of all ages, background and experiences. I, too, have been at the same crossroad, wondering if the path I choose should be safe and comfortable, or one that defies all that! I chose the path of defiance because safe and comfortable would not lead me to financial freedom. Historically, real estate has been a male-dominated industry and I cannot wait to be a part of this movement that will disrupt that.

—*Tina Somsith*
Small Business Owner/Real Estate Investor

TABLE OF CONTENTS

JOIN THE FLIPCHICK SISTERHOOD TODAY!

This book is only the beginning of your love affair with your money, yourself and your new real estate lifestyle. There is a whole lot more fun for you over at www. FlipChickCoaching.com

Ongoing support and community are critical for success in any area of your life. One of the biggest factors in our own ongoing success and wealth-building has been the posse of women holding one another accountable, being guides for each other, cheering one another on and supporting each other's goals and dreams. We want this for you, too.

We've put together resources, education, programs, tools, and ongoing support for you. Join us at www. FlipChickCoaching.com and learn how you can:

1. Join our exclusive community. Connect with other people reading the book and experiencing results. Ask questions. Give answers. Build wealth in community.

2. Do the exercises. Download PDFs of all the exercises in the book plus additional resources.

3. Access exclusive webinars, videos, programs, recommendations, interviews and articles. The material in this book is living and breathing in our own lives. As we build the community and continue to build our own wealth and yours, we will be sure to share these updates with you on the site.

4. Share your success. Share your own story of building wealth and discovering real estate. Read other people's stories to keep you inspired.

Visit www.FlipChickCoaching.com to join in the fun and go deeper with the book.

INTRODUCTION

Welcome to the FlipChick sisterhood! If you're like most modern women, you are yearning to be financially independent but you just aren't there yet. You may also have taken on some limiting money beliefs and common wealth misconceptions at some point in your life—beliefs such as, *It's not okay to make a lot of money,* or *It's not okay to **enjoy** making money.* How many of you have heard things like "Money doesn't grow on trees," or the often misquoted Bible passage, "The love of money is the root of all kinds of evil?" These mantras that many of us heard growing up were lies! Technically speaking, money IS made from trees, and loving money is a great idea! We can love having it, love the difference we can make with it, and love the amazing experiences we can have when there's enough leftover after paying rent to go out on a hot date, bliss out at the spa, or spend the afternoon at the amusement park with the kids.

> "The best way to help the poor is not to become one of them."
> **– Lang Hancock**

> "Money at its very essence is energy and all energy can be attracted or repelled."
> **– Andrea Bolder**

How many of you were also raised to believe that women cannot be financially independent? All of these

1

limiting beliefs take so many women and hold them captive. The fact is, money is an unlimited resource. Money is energy – and it moves in cycles based on the value you create and the value you desire. Loving and being grateful for all the money that is in your life and is already on its way to you today is a fantastic way to attract more of it into your life. When you create enough energy from the value you add to people and to the community, money flows freely and easily to you.

Take, for example, a situation I was in; I had seven flips going on at the same time, and wasn't able to sell a couple of the properties. I was thinking, "I have no money in my bank. How am I going to pay my mortgage, when all of my assets are in real estate?" Unexpectedly, I then got a call, "Hey, Margaret, I have $90,000 dollars, can I transfer it to you and get a high interest rate on it?" There are people out there who have underperforming money that they are looking to invest; there are banks that are sitting with millions of dollars that they need to loan out so that they can make more of it back. When you put the intention out there that money is easy, it's amazing how quickly and from how many places it flows.

You can be financially independent, and you don't have to wait until "someday." Actually, the only time you can start is now… today! That's all we've got, right?

It's time for a new approach. It's time to let go and OWN IT, ladies! Your beliefs have the power to launch your ideal life or to hold you back from your dreams. It's just a matter of choosing. I know you're ready, competent and able to break out of any old patterns keeping you from the wealth and financial independence you deserve, and I want to get you thinking about all the possibilities that are waiting for you once you do. Remember this if nothing else: Choosing the life you love and choosing to OWN IT, takes a heartbeat. No waiting is required.

In this book, I'll share a few personal stories and lessons members of my tribe—FlipChicks—have learned along the way about building wealth in real estate. My intention is to inspire and motivate you and have you become part of our community, the FlipChick sisterhood. I'll share the stories of three women, each unique in her situation, all of whom are seeking the same goal. As you read through the book, you will watch these women transform themselves as they journey towards financial independence. Before I share their stories, however, you're probably wondering about mine.

So what's my story? I grew up in the suburbs of Chicago, with parents who didn't really know or understand entrepreneurship or how to build wealth. They did what everyone taught back then: Go to school, get a good job, and then work hard. The idea was that the harder you work, the more money you make. Did you hear that same programming growing up?

By the time I was in high school, I was already looking for another avenue. I didn't want to end up like my parents—working hard, always living paycheck to paycheck, refinancing their home to pay off credit card debt. However, during my first semester of college, I found out I was pregnant. I got married and began working various jobs during the day and taking classes at night. It was tough. I was always struggling and trading time for money. The routine took its toll on me, and I ended up divorced by the time I was 21.

After graduation, I got a job in information technology. Enter the mind-numbing 9-to-5 phase of my life. Just thinking about how trapped I felt in that hours-driven, boring lifestyle is nauseating. No freedom and little money. I'd come home with no time or energy to give to my growing family. To everyone on the outside, we were living the American dream. Business was good. We usually had money left at the end of the month. What you couldn't see from the outside was the fact that I was working sometimes eighteen-hour days and someone else was kissing my kids goodnight.

That's when I decided to become a real estate investor. I was obsessed with those home flipping shows on TV, and I knew I was at least as smart as those guys. I read the book, *Rich Dad Poor Dad,* and I started asking everyone I knew if they had ever flipped a house or owned rental properties. My friends, it turned out, were not very savvy when it came to wealth building.

Instead, I learned by making a lot of mistakes. I wouldn't wish my experiences on anyone—which is a huge reason that I wrote this book. I don't want you to have to struggle to figure it out like I did.

I started flipping houses back in 2004. I thought it was pretty great when I made $20,000 on my first deal, but what I didn't know is that a monkey could make money in real estate in 2004. I was ignorance on fire. Not a good thing. I then bought a condo in 2006. I thought $300,000 was an insane amount of money to pay for a condo, but everyone was doing it, right? Well, I still own that condo, and just two years later the developer was bankrupt and the property appraised for $120,000. Ouch!

I wasn't ready to give up on real estate after my mistake, but I learned a valuable lesson. Get a coach! I began studying personal development with a series of very successful mentors, while also learning all I could about wealth creation and real estate investing with my boots on the ground. I also created an action plan—it's amazing, the power of drawing out your plan. It may have been a simple cartoon drawing, but it was the very first version of my success map which made it easier and easier to navigate my next winning steps.

All of these steps led me to creating a precise formula for finding a flipping sweet spot—the formula that I teach to my clients in the FlipChick sisterhood. Here's an exercise for you: Take a look at a few of the recent projects I've done in my real estate investing business.

Now, take a moment and imagine what it would feel like if these were your flips—if you were already an investor following the steps that I teach. Can you imagine it? What does it feel like? How would your world change?

Even though I've flipped more than 100 properties like these, (a couple hundred transactions including

rentals), I still get excited each time I take on a new project. It feels like I'm getting into a game that I'm certain I can win. Real estate has allowed me to live a fulfilling and freedom-driven lifestyle—and I want the same for you.

I wrote this book to illustrate how easy it is to begin creating the life you love and deserve, by flipping real estate. Being a FlipChick equals freedom. It can give you the freedom to go on a vacation and pay for your friends or family to come with. It can give you the freedom to spend more quality time with your kids. It can give you the freedom to be with the ones you love and care about, especially in their times of need. It can give you the freedom to tap into your creativity and feel fully alive, like the genius you are. Now that I have financial freedom and my family is taken care of, I get to give back in a way I never imagined possible. In 2014, I opened a home for teen moms and babies who were victims of rape. All of this and more is possible for you, too.

As you embark on your own FlipChick journey, the first thing you need to know is this: *It's okay to make money*. It's okay to make money! Let's take that one step further. You MUST make money, because money is the measure of the value you are giving to the world.

I once received a very long personal email from a woman who had attended one of my webinars; she said, "I don't have a dime in my bank. Could you mentor me and make sure that I'm successful in my first flip?" My answer to that is, "No." Anybody who's focused on lack and not the value she could offer that would cause money spent to come back to her, is not someone that will be successful in my program. If you want more money, you have to circulate more money. It's like a snowball; you have to start pushing the snowball so it can grow. If you keep your little snowball in your hand, it's going to melt.

Now, keep in mind that in some parts of the world and in different cultures, money can come in the form of services, experiences and other emotional reward systems. In other words, it's okay to get an incredible return on the investments you make with your life energy.

Take a breath and let this sink in: It's okay to make, love, give and circulate money. In fact, it's more than okay to make money. You want to make a difference in the world; you want to stop abuse, you want to feed the hungry, but how are you going to do that without resources? Nothing is going to change if you continue on without expanding your resources. You might be in the position where you can direct other people's resources in a helpful way, but ultimately, the people who have the resources will continue to be the ones who determine the direction of society. It's the Golden Rule…she who has the gold makes the rules.

Here's the real secret about money: No matter who you are, money is just going to make you more of who you are. If you're a rotten person and you don't contribute anything, it doesn't matter if you have ten dollars or ten million dollars, you're still a rotten person who doesn't contribute anything. Please know that you can be a wealthy woman without having to be a self-centered, "money-driven" woman. And whether you have ten dollars or ten million dollars, you can make a world of difference as a classy, empowered and selfLESS woman.

Having more money allows you to help more people. And by help I don't just mean give it away. I've added numerous rental properties to my portfolio, which means there are many families living in nice homes, homes made possible because of the business I've created. The FlipChick sisterhood employs many contractors who wouldn't typically work year-round; those contractors are grateful every Christmas because these women keep them working throughout the year.

To be clear, in this book, I'm not writing about hoarding money. Money sitting in a bank or stuffed in your mattress doesn't accomplish anything. It's not about accumulating for the sake of accumulating. Your money needs to be working for you. Back to the "love of money" misconception…who has the energy to love an inanimate object that can't even take out the trash? It's about being a good steward of the money; when you are a good steward of your money, then you can make a difference. Remember, money has little to no value, unless it's leveraged or circulating. It must be moving and living to have real, residual value. Nobody on their deathbed wishes they had another million just sitting in the bank, that they never did anything with. This book and the FlipChick sisterhood goes beyond just helping other people, it is about helping yourself, too. You actually can't take care of other people unless you can take care of yourself first.

Real estate is a powerful way to invest your money so that it is continually earning for you. The more money your investments bring you, the more you can choose what you do, where you do it and who you do it with. That's what true freedom looks like. It is no longer just about what you're earning; it's about how you manage and grow your money. It's not just about getting rich; it's about staying wealthy. There's a big difference between earning and investing, and between creating income and building residual income, which we'll talk about later.

In this book, I'm going to share my one approach to investing that I have found incredibly lucrative in my own life, which is why I want to share it with you. I want to empower you to become a financially independent woman, because with a sisterhood of FlipChicks who are financially independent and generous-minded, we truly can change the world in a profound way - together.

This book is designed to help you start to see how you can not only become financially independent, but actually grow a wealth portfolio that is self-sustaining. We do this through investing. The ebb and flow of life should be supported by your investments. "Ebb and flow" is defined as "coming and going," or "decline and regrowth." Life happens, people get divorced, lose their jobs, have sick kids or parents. It's not a matter of *if* the ebb will happen, it's when.

When I found out I was pregnant, I had nothing. I could have decided not to become a mom, or to drop out of school. But I decided that my current life circumstances were temporary—and irrelevant to where I was going. I was determined to finish school and to be financially independent. I couldn't have been more grateful for my commitment to that path than when I got a phone call several years later that my mom was going into the emergency room. This time, I had a system already in place and sufficient enough income so that for the next two months—the last two months of my mom's life—I didn't have to think about work.

The question you need to ask yourself is, "Am I prepared for the ebbs and flows of life?" It's our job in this book to make your answer not just "yes," but a resounding "HELL YEAH – BRING IT ON!!" During the flows of life, it's time to prepare, plan, invest and cushion your "landing" for the ebbs. It just makes sense to look ahead and anticipate those times when you'll need that extra support. And, this all comes about by looking ahead and being proactive – in advance of the times when your flow wanes a bit.

Many people fluctuate between trying to save for a rainy day…emphasis on *trying,* and dipping into that savings when it rains. What's even worse is that most people don't even have the savings to dip into, so they fall into debt, which is very difficult (but not impossible, and certainly easier with our wealth building strategies) to get out from under. A savvy FlipChick invests for a rainy day by investing in an asset that taps into the compounding machine. You will never need to tap into savings, because you OWN IT, the power of compounding is working for you and protecting you from the negative impact most will feel from the ebb and flow of life. We'll go deep with compounding later on in Part 4, "Money," but for now, know that compounding is the most important wealth-building principle you will learn—and once you apply it, you will have the life of your dreams. Did you hear that? THE MOST IMPORTANT principle…and we're going to teach you what it is, and how you will apply it to build your own wealth machine.

Living on investments isn't the worst thing you can do. If you have investments to live on, you're doing pretty well. If you have to tap into your investments, the compounding happens in reverse, too. (Again, more on that later.) If you pull money out of something that grew by compounding, you're pulling away from something that took time to build, and when left untouched becomes quite literally like your own ATM machine. But if you break the machine, it's devastating to your cash flow and long-term wealth. Review the story of the Golden Goose for a refresher on why you DON'T KILL THE GOOSE. If this sounds complicated, don't worry. It isn't, once you have a better understanding of the basic principals of compounding.

My number one goal is to help you tap into the power of compounding, to get in line and stay in line, to minimize, or dare I say *eliminate* financial worry– so that's reason to relax, grab a hot cup of tea (or beverage of choice) and read on!

Three Women, Three Stories

To help you get excited about the possibilities – and the steps you might take along the way – here are the stories of three very ordinary women who made their way to having a life of extraordinary financial independence through real estate investing.

Each of these women are in their own unique situation when it comes to career, stage of life, amount they earn, and relationship status, yet they all have one thing in common: the desire to break free of their patterns and achieve the life of their dreams. They all started with no experience in real estate or investing, and learned how to take control of their finances, how to leverage real estate investing in different ways, and how to transform their lives in the process. Maybe you'll recognize a bit of yourself in one – or all three – of these stories.

Teacher Tara

I know the day everything changed for me was a Tuesday, because Tuesday is the day I leave school early so I can pick up my dry cleaning.

All of my life had been very predictable. I did everything in the right order. I graduated from college at 22. I got my teaching certificate at 23. I got a job instantly, teaching sixth grade at a middle school in the town I grew up in. I was secure, safe and deeply entrenched in my comfort zone.

My big, mapped-out life plans said I would buy my first home at 24, get married at 25, and have my first baby at 28. Instead, I celebrated my 25th birthday single, and loving every minute of it. Although I was renting, I lived on my own in a beautiful condo, I had a new car that I paid cash for, money in the bank, and I was the envy of both my corporate friends and my stay-at-home-mom friends who couldn't seem to stop talking about foreign concepts like dirty diapers and breast pumps. I spent my summers trying out all the

DIY projects I saw on Pinterest, and entertained on the weekends, since most of my friends had one of those dreaded 9-to-5, year-round jobs. I often felt sorry for my corporate friends who had to work all summer while I was enjoying my time off, or my mom friends who said they sometimes lock themselves in the bathroom just to have five minutes to themselves. The truth was, even though I had rampant free time, I never really embarked on any notable adventures. My limited excursions into "adventure" included socializing with my friends, hitting the beach with a good book for a few days, or just heading out on a shopping spree, but nothing more.

As I drove to the dry cleaners on that particular Tuesday, I reflected back on an email that had been randomly delivered to my inbox that morning. I'm a girl who likes routine; I arrive early at work, pour my half-caf with vanilla cream and one packet of raw sugar, I settle into my desk and check my email. Like everyone, I get a lot of junk in my inbox. For some reason, one email caught my eye that day. It advertised an online real estate investing course.

Now, you have to know, I have always been financially secure. I am the one without kids, the one who has all the nice things. I go to yoga class, I have a personal trainer, I eat organic. My friends with kids envy me and my perceived disposable income. I'm not lavish, but I do have nice clothes, nice home decor, a fully-stocked kitchen, all of those "finer things." I never complain or lament about being broke. I also love my job, a rarity these days it seems, at least amongst my friends. I never complain. I enjoy teaching. I didn't go into teaching for the money, security or pension – I did it because I love to teach. I love interacting with kids every day, I teach the best grade of all, and have always felt fulfilled.

Despite all this, there were times I still felt restless, because I knew I could be doing more with my money. I watched TV most nights and heard bits and spurts about financial advice. I got a kick out of watching Suze Orman berate the financially clueless, and I'm pretty sure she would have given a thumbs up to all the financial decisions I'd made. I felt confident that I was being smart about saving and spending, but I didn't know a thing about investing, and none of my friends did, either.

> "Money is a living entity, and it responds to energy exactly the same way you do. It is drawn to those who welcome it, those who respect it. Wouldn't you rather be with people who respect you and who don't want you to be something you're not? Your money feels the same way."
> – **Suze Orman**

My parents would constantly badger me to make sure I had enough retirement savings. I didn't worry about retirement since I had a teachers' pension. But I did have this little voice, wondering if there was something better, different, or more that I could be doing with my money.

It was the third email I opened, and usually I would send it straight to the trash folder, but something in the subject caught my attention. This time my mind said "What if?" I thought it must be some cosmic joke that for the third time in a week, I was faced with questioning if I was meant to be doing more with my money. It wasn't the promise of getting rich in the subject line that caught my eye in that email; it was the promise of something new - a shift and a new way of thinking. Just a few nights before, I was flipping through the television, and I heard some stories of people getting rich flipping homes. I chuckled and thought, yeah right. But that small voice in my head said, "Is it possible?" Ironically, over the weekend, I'd had a few girls over for game night, and one shared a story about her cousin, who had started buying homes to fix and flip with her husband, and they just sold their second property. I was shocked to think someone in the real world, not just on TV, could be doing this, but more than shocked, I was intrigued. How much fun would that be to spend a summer fixing up a house? Talk about a DIY project; now THAT would be fun. I was curious, but who was I kidding? I couldn't do that. "You need a partner to do that," I thought. "I can't do something like that alone; she has a husband to help her."

I opened the email and scanned the contents. I clicked on a link and landed on a page talking about the course. The bell rang before I could read the page. I snapped the computer shut, and headed into the hall. Kids were everywhere, running to class. I entered the classroom to see thirty faces smiling at me.

When class was over for the day, I lingered at my desk a while. Some of the kids were waiting to be picked up, and I let them wait in the classroom so they didn't have to stand with the "big kids" on the front steps.

After all the children had been picked up and the classroom was tidied, I drove to the dry cleaners, thinking about real estate. Could I be like one of those people on TV who flipped houses? Could I find my own path to investing like my friend's cousin? What a funny thought. I couldn't stop thinking about it. I felt excited, and I didn't know why. I couldn't wait to read about the course. Maybe this was just the thing I had been looking for. Maybe this was one of those times where the very answers I'd been looking for… the very steps I needed to take for adventure, change and excitement in my life… were on the other side of this course application? I'd seen courses in the past that didn't really excite me… but for some reason, my inspiration compass was pointing me toward making a move into the unknown – into something I'd never done before.

Corporate Cathy

I drove to the office down the same streets I had driven for the past 12 years, except this time I drove right past the office to the park three blocks further. I felt the same heavy, sick feeling I had grown accustomed to between 8 and 9 a.m. My babies no longer cried when mommy left. At 9 and 11 years old, they had long since gotten used to walking themselves to the bus stop and letting themselves in through the garage after school.

Today something was different. Maybe it was the pizza I ate while finishing up my expansion plan at 9 p.m. last night. Maybe it was the guilt of missing my daughter's tennis match on Tuesday. Maybe it was classic midlife crisis, but today something in me snapped. I recalled a fact that I had recently heard on a podcast, that 70% of working Americans hate their jobs. It was in that moment that I realized I had become a statistic.

I couldn't do it anymore. I couldn't clock into the prison of my 9-to-5 job and lock myself into my cubicle. I couldn't miss another tennis match. I couldn't order another pizza dinner because I'd be working late again. I was determined to look at my past regrets and commit to start living a life that I loved, to spend time with my kids, to travel, to do what's on my bucket list. My thoughts spun around what I would no longer do, what I would no longer tolerate in my world. Who was I kidding; I never made a bucket list. I didn't have time to make a bucket list.

So that's where I started. I deliberately missed the turn to the office. I remembered the podcast saying that the best way to make a change is to do it *now*. So, I changed. I missed my turn.

Rather than pulling into my prison cell of a parking spot, I pulled into the park just up the street. It was 9 a.m. on a weekday morning and the only people in the park were mommies and nannies. I was never one of those moms. My kids went to the park with our nanny. I teared up a bit at the thought of it; I had never taken my kids to a park on a weekday when they were toddlers. How much time had I given up to work?

I sat on a park bench beneath a large oak tree, and pulled out my notebook. It was time to make my bucket list. I wrote for a while, and came up with a list of 100 things. Hiking in New Zealand. Touring the wineries of Chile. Taking a hot air balloon ride in Nevada. Seeing the pyramids. When I was done, I felt… okay. I put it away. It was only 10 a.m. Now what?

I went home. I changed out of my work clothes. Slowly, a feeling of freedom was coming over me. The kids would be with their dad for the night, so I had the whole day.

Not used to having time to myself, I started by catching up on laundry and dishes; I even packed up my off-season clothes. I was feeling quite accomplished until I realized it was after 2 p.m. and I still hadn't eaten lunch. I thought I would just quickly check email, then take full advantage of what remained of my day playing hooky. I filtered through my junk email first; I receive a lot of newsletters, particularly from coaches. What can I say? I watch Oprah. I love Super Soul Sunday. I've become a bit of a personal development junkie; I get daily emails from no less than a dozen mentors and coaches. I like them, but I never take them up on their offers to "change my life."

Until today, that is. One offer caught my attention. It was a financial coach, working in my city. I don't know if it was the words, or the way she said them, or just my mood, but after I read the email, suddenly I found myself on a website and even more suddenly, I was clicking "Yes" to an offer for a free coaching session.

I got up from the computer, prepared a big salad, and opened a bottle of wine. I was looking forward to a peaceful night. No kids meant I had control of the TV, and no work meant I could actually just veg out and watch TV.

No sooner had I sat down with my wine than my phone rang.

"Hello?"

"Is this Cathy?" a woman's voice on the other end asked.

"Yes, who's this?"

"Hi Cathy, my name is Maggie. I'm just calling to follow up with your request for coaching this afternoon."

"Oh! Hello," that was fast, I thought, "Thanks for calling!"

"Is now a good time?" Maggie asked.

I took a sip of wine and felt the warmth and flavor calm me instantly. "Sure," I said, settling into my white leather sofa with my glass of wine.

Maggie began to explain more about the coaching I had signed up for. She explained that with their program and help, I could not only pay off debt but create passive income – a term I wasn't familiar with, but Maggie explained simply as making money while I slept. That definitely sounded good.

This time, I listened. I listened and I sipped wine. Despite being tipsy from drinking on an empty stomach, as I had not touched my salad yet, I was clear in my mind. This coach was talking directly to me. The little bits of info I had filled out on the form earlier were enough for her to know exactly what I needed to hear and also, to feel. As I listened, I felt like the shift I had been praying for all day was arriving. She was showing me a way out, a way into something new. Although I knew she was showing me something new, what I didn't realize at the time was that she was actually showing me the first steps on my path to freedom. By the time we hung up, I had a plan, calls scheduled, videos coming to me, and an entirely new course of action.

I was excited. But I was tired. I turned on the TV, put my feet up, and spent the evening drinking wine with my guilty pleasure, reality television. I had a deep sense of inner peace that came from what my coach explained as feeling the early results of new action. Although I had only taken one small step, by contacting a coach, I was now moving in a direction, down a new path that had eluded me for my entire life. I could already feel new doors opening for me.

Retired Rebecca

The flight was particularly turbulent, but our captain expertly landed us. I held a young girl's hand as the plane bounced around, trying to keep her calm. After 30 years of flying, it wasn't turbulence that scared me. It was the thought of retirement.

I was in my final days at the airline and wondering about money. I had worked as a flight attendant for 30 years. Fresh out of college at 21, I got a job right away. Same job, same airline for 30 years. Some people would say I was lucky enough to have emerged from a full 30-year career of flying alive, but I didn't see it that way. What I did see was the cutting of pensions, year after year, and now that I was eager to retire, there was very little left in the pension pot for me to claim.

I had been working the same job and married to the same man for 30 years. I looked around and wondered just where my life had gone? Two of my kids had grown up and were out of the house. My oldest daughter had been living overseas for the last two years; every time we'd call, she would be on a new adventure. I think I lived vicariously through her. I had become a flight attendant because I had that same sense of adventure my oldest daughter had; I wanted to travel. I can't deny that I got to travel. It was just a different kind of traveling, that in the end I didn't find fulfilling. Then there was my second oldest, our only son, who had a beautiful wife and children. My third was finishing college. She wanted to be an entrepreneur, like her father.

My husband had owned his own business since we were in our 30s. We joked that it seemed like the business owned him most of the time. A few years ago, we realized that if he wasn't actively showing up working in his business to collect a check, we wouldn't be able to survive more than a few months. At our age, that was a scary thought. It's not that he's bad with money, it's just that he saw the company as his investment. He was passionate about his business and every penny went back into the business. Our big retirement plan was to sell the company when he was ready to stop working. Now, however, it seemed that our daughter might follow in his footsteps and take over the company, so it didn't look like a big cash-out would happen. It became clear that the way we were headed, we would be left with more life at the end of our money after we retired.

I felt ready to retire; I felt energized at the thought of it. I just didn't know how we were going to find the money to do what we needed to do. I wanted to travel, to explore, even if it was in an RV across North America.

My husband didn't share my enthusiasm for travel, but I know he'd go with me wherever it was. The question was, how could we possibly make it happen? This was the time when the excuses began to flow... that the fear in the pit of my stomach began to creep in.

I had been thinking about that predicament for a few days when the solution landed literally at my feet. I do a lot of charity work, and I was volunteering at a charity event— a dinner and fundraiser for breast cancer research. I had a moment between greeting women at the information desk that I saw something drop out of one woman's bag as she walked by. It fluttered and landed at my feet. I picked it up and wanted to call out to her, but she was gone into the sea of women. I read the paper. It was an invitation to a free seminar. The topic? *How to Create Passive Income through Real Estate.*

Hmmm, I thought to myself. I folded the invitation, and tucked it into my purse. I knew I would go. There was no question. Today there was no room for excuses. Today, I was the version of me that could not allow any excuse or obstacle to get in my way. Yup, no question at all.

MINDSET

Mindset plays the biggest role in establishing a solid foundation for wealth creation. You wouldn't dare build a house without a foundation, so don't dare skip this step when building your wealth castle. Take an honest assessment of your mindset. Do you think positively? Glass half-full kinda girl? Or do negative thoughts take over your mind throughout the day such as, *Why does this always happen to me? Must be nice to have...* (insert whatever desire you think you should have but don't—a wealthy husband, big house, family close by, kids/no kids, etc.).

Shifting from negative to positive, believing in yourself, knowing you can change... all of these things are fundamental to becoming a financially independent woman. Believe it or not, understanding and applying the concepts in this chapter constitutes the most important part of the wealth accumulation process. In this chapter are critical ideas and tips to help you see where your mind can use a shift, and learn how to support these shifts.

Growing and improving ourselves is all about taking these small steps. We FlipChicks know this from our own experience. For me, it wasn't until I took my own development seriously and began doing the work required to shift my mindset that I saw just how available change was for me. And my FlipChick success sure didn't happen overnight. This section is all about the basic first steps anyone can take to change their mindset – and set the foundation for a life of financial independence.

> "Thoughts become things. If you see it in your mind, you will hold it in your hand."
> – **Bob Proctor**

A. Get Clear on Your Values

At the basis of mindset are our values. Carefully consider just how vital it is to get clear on your values. When you start to lead your life based on your values, this is when critical change happens. Do you have a handle on what you value most? When opportunities come your way, are you fully prepared to make your decisions based

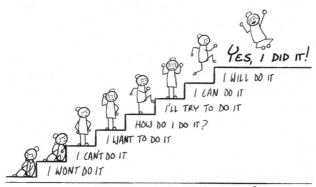

YES, I DID IT!

I WILL DO IT

I CAN DO IT

I'LL TRY TO DO IT

HOW DO I DO IT?

I WANT TO DO IT

I CAN'T DO IT

I WON'T DO IT

WHICH STEP HAVE YOU REACHED TODAY?

on what matters most? Your values are your ruler… they must rule the choices you make. Otherwise, you'll find yourself moving in the direction of instant gratification, pleasure and convenience – or even worse, short-term gains that will yield long-term failures.

We all have those lists of things we want more of in our lives, right? And maybe even a bigger list of things we want less of. At the basis of these are our values. We all have

> *"It's not hard to make decisions once you know what your values are."*
> **– Roy E. Disney**

"toward values" and "away values." For example, my "toward values" are: time with family, financial security, living an exciting, adventurous life, freedom, flexibility, and efficiency. My "away values" are: chaos, being told what to do, dependence/needing to rely on somebody else, not being able to influence the outcome.

Are you sufficiently motivated to move toward positive values? Are you clear on the values you want to move away from? When you know what you want to move toward, and what you want to move away from, the process of change becomes quite simple.

Both Tara and Cathy did some work around values at the beginning of their journey. Let's look first at an example of sufficient motivation that caused Tara to make a big change in her life, and then at Cathy's values assessment. At the end of this chapter, there is an exercise that will help you define both your toward and your away values.

Teacher Tara

Since my course was online, I could begin anytime. I chose to begin on a Saturday in March. Spring was in the air, and what better time to start something new? Added to the fresh sense of spring was that new voice in me that kept repeating, "Wow, look at what you're doing! You are no longer predictable. You've made a choice and that choice could very well change the course of your life."

The first exercise was about determining values. I read through the exercise, a little surprised that we weren't just launching into investing strategies right away. The first section of the course, instead, was about determining values and setting goals in alignment with these values. It also covered standards and how to put my "stakes in the ground" in order to make my life and business decisions stick – so I could both respect myself and be respected by those around me.

Hmmmm. I thought to myself as I read about "toward values" and "away values." I thought back in my life to the times when I made choices to get away from something – like when I finally decided to move out of my parents' home. Putting that decision in the context of what I was learning, my toward values were freedom, independence, growing my self-confidence. The away values – and the ones that played the strongest part at the time – were getting away from my mother's nagging, and my father's obnoxious comments. Not having to listen to the football game all the time also fell into this category.

I began to separate out what I was really working toward versus what I was just trying to get away from by taking this course. The more I read and learned, the more I realized that focusing on the toward values is far more satisfying than the away values. I also found more toward values to list; the more I listed, the more excitement awakened inside of me as I imagined the possibilities. These values included financial independence, and being able to donate both my time and money— having money put away to retire with and giving freely to causes I believed in. Just like my move from my parents' home, much of my toward values came down to freedom and confidence. I also learned that the away values are fear-based, the toward values are future-based. Once I focused more on the toward values, I instantly felt more motivated and hopeful to really do this course fully.

Corporate Cathy

I took to the coaching like a fish to water. Sure, it was difficult making changes at first and doing the exercises, but my coach held me accountable, which kept me going. Each of the exercises my coach assigned gave me an entirely new window into my life and behavior, and really began to give me hope. I was getting to really know *me*, the version of me I always hoped I could be.

In the early days, we worked with values. What was I moving toward, what was I moving away from? I knew I was moving toward spending more time with my kids, more time with my girlfriends, more time to exercise, more security, more stability, more fun in my life, and less pressure. In short, more fulfillment from each moment rather than always looking for the distraction or project at work to busy me so I could get through to the next vacation, long weekend or day off.

I needed to move away from the stress, and working for somebody else. I wanted to move away from an obligation to somebody else's time clock. I wanted to move away from the control that my boss had on my life. As I wrote my lists, it seemed there was much more that I wanted to move away from. It was overwhelming.

Maggie redirected me, and suggested we focus on what I wanted to move towards. Much simpler, and it made me feel happier too.

This work reminded me of my divorce and it brought up some of the raw emotion that I still had lingering. Even though I had been divorced for over two years, there was still a lot that had not been resolved. This work I was doing on myself revealed to me just how much I had been living in the clouds. By this, I mean, I was thinking only one way about everything.

I remember being on a flight with my daughter, where we took off in a bumpy rain storm. She looked at me, her eyes wide with fear, and I explained to her that this storm was just something we would be passing through. We were looking out the windows and all we could see was the rain and clouds; we were in the thick of it, but it was only temporary. The bumps, the rain, the drama, it's all temporary. We just had to go through it on our way to the place above the clouds where the sun was shining. Sure enough, the pilot took us up above the storm, and we were no longer in the clouds. We could now see the situation from a different perspective, a higher perspective.

Although I was the wise one that day on the airplane, it took working with a coach for me to see the storms in my own life from a different perspective. I realized that lately I had gotten so caught up with what was in front of me, that I had forgotten that on the other side of all the clouds, the sun was still shining.

Both Tara and Cathy were able to get clear on their values by doing the values clarification exercise, and this type of clarity is an essential component of becoming free. If we are not clear on our toward and away values, we inevitably end up making choices that are fear-based. It seems for many of us first doing this exercise, we spend more time moving away from fear-based values—fears that we can't be very successful, that we'll always live paycheck to paycheck, that we cannot pay for our kids' college, that we can't fix a broken-down car, or that we can't have what we want to have in life. It is important to focus more on moving toward the values that reflect our highest and best possible life.

Clarifying values is a must to reach success. There's no judgment of values, it's personal and individual, but we must be clear on our values. Our values are our WHY: Why do you want more freedom? Why is financial independence important to you? Our why is our driving force, our reason. Our why is what we need to keep us going when the going gets tough.

TOWARD/AWAY VALUES EXERCISE	
This is what I want to move toward	This is what I want to move away from

Notice that all the "move away froms" are fear-based.

B. Circle of Influence: Beware the Naysayers

Are you where you want to be in life? Are you taking advice from people who are where you want to go? If I can give you one word of advice, it's this: Don't take advice from people just because they are your next door neighbors or your relatives. Don't take advice from people who are living in the same situation that you are in;

> "Hey, I found your nose.
> It was in my business
> again."
> **– Anonymous**

rather, take it from the people who are now living the life that they want to be living; a life more in line with what *you* want to be living.

Reality TV shows on flipping houses weren't as prevalent in 2006 when I started in real estate as they are today. When I started, people were trying to give me all kinds of unsolicited advice, even though some of them had never even flipped any homes or tried to build a real estate flipping business. I'm not just talking about unsolicited advice, but advice from unqualified advice-givers.

I had no experience flipping homes when I began, but I'd seen people on TV who said they'd made as much in a deal as the average person makes in a year, so I thought, "Why not? I'll try it. I have no idea if I'll fail, or if I'll be super successful. But I'll try it." I began with no construction experience, and no financing experience. I learned through trial and error. With every house I flipped, I learned something new. I didn't know there were coaches or training programs on real estate—I simply asked myself, "What do I need to do next? Oh, electrical, okay. I can find an electrician. Oh, look, there's water coming out of the walls. I guess I need a plumber now." If I'd had an experienced coach or a mentor from day one, I would have saved myself a lot of time and money. Instead, I had people around me who had never done what I was doing—telling me that I didn't know what I was doing. For example, a family member insisted that I would never make any money if I didn't hire union labor; I had learned through experience that the opposite was true—I'd never make money if I paid everybody $150 an hour.

Beware the Naysayers. I'm happy with unsolicited advice if you've made billions, or even tens of millions. Sure, go ahead, bend my ear! Otherwise, I'm all set, thank you very much.

> "The person who says it cannot be done should not interrupt the person doing it."
> **– Chinese Proverb**

How can you practice filtering advice that doesn't truly provide you value? Easy… consider the source. If someone offers you advice, feel free to be polite and listen, unless you can move away from the conversation politely. But, always mentally note that regardless of what this person says to you, if you don't know for certain that they have had great success in this area – move on to more reliable sources.

Also, never let outside influences stop you from pursuing your dreams and moving forward. I've seen unsolicited advice stop many people dead in their tracks. This becomes especially true if you have a strong attachment to pleasing others, including family members, parents or others who are close to you.

I had a girl take one of my classes, who asked us not to post pictures we'd taken of her on Facebook because she didn't want her sister to know she'd attended. When she'd told her sister she'd registered for the class, her sister said, "How can you be so irresponsible? It's like gambling." This particular woman ended up becoming a realtor; she still hasn't flipped houses because she was afraid of what her sister would think of her.

> "When people seek to undermine your dreams, predict your doom or criticize you, remember that they are telling you their story, not yours."
> – Cynthia Occelli

Of course, our family members and friends mean well in their warnings of doom and gloom. But, this is their way of projecting their fears, excuses and failures, or lack of action on you. Don't take it in! Or ask yourself, "Is this true? Can I be sure that it's true? If it isn't true, then how could the opposite be true? Does this apply to me?" Usually the best and first step is to just let unsolicited advice go in one ear and out the next, without giving any energy to it. Cathy nearly didn't follow through signing up with her coach because of the unsolicited advice of her girlfriends. Let's see how she handled it.

Corporate Cathy

I was out to lunch with my girlfriends, mainly old friends from the office. The more I was away from that environment, the more I became aware that those relationships were built on superficial grounds. Still, I engaged in a social lunch with them every so often, mostly out of habit. They were my friends and in some ways a support group for the twenty years we all worked together. I couldn't just abandon them, could I?

I felt that way up until one particular lunch experience. After that, I knew I might have to start being more selective with my friendships. All their unsolicited advice was coming my way and clouding my head.

I had just made the decision to begin coaching with Maggie that morning. I was the first to arrive to the restaurant, and I felt good. I felt empowered, as if just deciding to work with a coach alone was enough to change me.

I knew the minute Lisa and Bev arrived that my good feeling would not last. How had I not noticed this, all these years? Lisa and Bev, in particular, were negative about everything. They gossiped, criticized, and had an opinion on everything. *Wow, had I been immersing myself in this unnecessary drama the entire time?* I wondered to myself.

Of course, I had been so excited to share my recent decision that I blurted it out right away. "I'm working with a coach!" I said as the white wine spritzers arrived.

Lisa took a sip and looked at Bev, who also took a sip of her drink. They did not have smiles on their faces. "What kind of coach?" Lisa asked. "You need to make sure they are certified."

I nodded. "Of course! Her name is Maggie. She's a life coach but also teaches money strategies."

"Huh, money strategies. Honey, every life coach is just a hack. Don't take investing advice from a coach. Seriously." Bev retorted, as if she'd had some sort of experience working with a coach that qualified her to share her opinion in this "helpful" way.

I began to get a sick feeling inside. Had I just committed thousands of dollars to a hack? Though my instincts had told me "no" when I talked to my coach, who was I to believe?

Bev began, "If you want my opinion, you should cancel the coaching and hire a financial advisor." That's what she did, and that's what everyone she knows does. Come to think of it, that's what most people I know do. But when I look at their lives, they look just like the life I was working to move away from. They didn't have financial freedom, they didn't indulge in regular vacations, they didn't get to spend more time with their kids.

"What about me gaining my own knowledge and experience so that I can make my own choices?" I felt myself becoming defensive. Who did these women think they were?

Lisa laughed. "Cathy, women don't do these things for themselves. Your coach will probably give you a bunch of useless exercises while she laughs and pockets the money. Seriously. You'd be better off just directly hiring a planner to invest your money – if that's what you want to do."

I decided to stop engaging the subject. I couldn't believe I had never noticed how negative and narrow-minded these two were. I realized I may have to slowly cut the toxic ties—or maybe it would be easier than I thought. I didn't care to have this conversation with these women anymore. I knew working with my coach was the best next step for me. I began mapping out my exit strategy in my mind, so I no longer exposed myself to these naysayers!

I have experienced far too many women like Cathy approach me with heads full of unsolicited advice that has them all rattled and confused. I don't want this to happen to you. I'm also not saying to do every single thing I say or take it as your perfect answer. All I can do is speak from my experience and share both my mistakes and lessons, as well as the steps I've taken to find my own success along the way.

Learn to trust your gut, because ultimately you know what's true and right for you. With practice and experience, you'll have a strong sense of the path to take, which is the reason I've written this book— to empower you to make choices that create the lifestyle you love. Don't let bad, unsolicited advice crowd your brain or waste your energy. At the end of the day, you know what to do. And when you choose to take action, don't let anything get in your way!

C. Personal Development

There's nobody as close to your life as you are. And, when you're that close, it's easy to miss the big picture. Remember the clouds surrounding the airplane? I've experienced and learned from this myself and want to share the lesson with you: More than 90% of navigation is course correction.

Much of life is as if you're taking an aircraft flight. You are heading for a destination: you are coming from one place and heading to another place. It requires navigation. Any time you are heading anywhere, you get sway—which means you get off course.

Say you are going from Los Angeles to New York, and you're flying one degree off course. Assuming you're one degree off in the northerly direction, by the time you end up on the east coast, you're going to be 150 to 200 miles north of New York, which could put you in Vermont. It could put you in New Hampshire. It could put you in the ocean.

It's been said that you can't read the label from inside the bottle. This is why it's important to have a mentor or a coach— someone who can see what you're doing from the outside. A coach will hold you accountable, remind you of your goals, and get you to reset and course correct so you're taking the action that's most important to you.

There's this false idea that somehow we can figure things out on our own and still have amazing success. But the truth is that all of us must reach outside of ourselves to really grow. Think of it this way: If you don't have access to insights, accountability and even guidance from resources outside of yourself, you may always do what you already know and what you've already done. Logic and the insanity test tells us that this path will give you the same results you've always gotten.

> "The purest form of insanity is to leave everything the same and the same time hope that things will change."
> **– Albert Einstein**

You MUST access outside guidance to truly grow and succeed in life at the level you desire. It's the very reason you're reading this book! I've had a coach for most of my entrepreneurial career and still have a coach today.

CIRCLE OF INFLUENCE EXERCISE

Who are the 5 people you most closely associate with? List their names and the following traits for each person: positive qualities, negative qualities, how they help me move toward my goals, how they prevent me from reaching my goals

1.

2.

3.

4.

5.

Make a list of 5 people you will proactively seek to connect with, then answer the following for each person: positive qualities, how they will encourage me, challenge me, help me reach my goals

1.

2.

3.

4.

5.

Imagine a professional sports figure trying to figure it all out without a coach. It's nonsense.

A truly fulfilled life requires constant improvement and progress. If we're not out there actively pursuing improvement, greatness or a better life, it won't happen. There is not one person in the world for whom this isn't true. And it doesn't happen by sitting in front of a television. It happens by reading books, taking courses, workshops, doing the work, and then... more important than anything, taking massive action in the direction of your dreams.

It's not difficult to see the evidence of this belief within any individual's life. Look at what choices he or she has been making on a regular basis. The compounded result of what people eat shows up in their physical appearance, as does their time spent at the gym versus their time spent in front of the television. You won't get a beer gut when you're eating a raw vegan diet and spending five days a week at the gym.

> *"Commit to CANI – Constant and never-ending improvement."*
> **– Anthony Robbins**

Likewise, you won't get rock hard abs by drinking a bottle of wine every night and spending five nights a week watching reality television. The books you read, how you spend your weekends, and who you spend your time with all contribute to the quality of your life. The evidence will show up in the quality of your relationships and your overall happiness. You've likely heard the expression, "If you're happy don't forget to tell your face." The evidence is very telling.

We can also look at somebody's bank account and know what they are doing with their money. They can say, "I'm smart with my money," but if they have $100 in their account and last month they were overdrawn, then they're not smart with their money or with their income creation system. In order to get to a place where they have $10,000 in the bank, then they have to make different choices than whatever they did to get $100 in the bank.

I've learned and know from experience and from making my own mistakes that continual growth and expansion is essential to leading a happy life. You don't even have to start out wanting to reach a huge, altruistic, higher purpose, either. As you go through the process of setting your goals, the personal development work you do inevitably leads you to fulfilling your higher purpose. And, it doesn't happen by taking 10,000 actions at a time. It comes from taking one very valuable action 10,000 times. Let's use the money example again. If we say, "I want to make $10,000 a month instead of $2,000 a month," it's not just a function of step one, step two, step three. It's not just mechanical and it isn't going to arrive from going after a dozen goals. First, you must focus on your top priority goals – and keep them few and specific. Then, there's a huge emotional side to the work, and that is one reason why women are so successful as real estate investors. It might begin with the simple question of, "What does money mean to me?"

Have you ever thought, "I'm a smart girl, but I'm stupid with money?"

Are you kidding me?

Please don't say that anymore because the more you say and think that (or practice any other self-limiting belief), the more it will become true. It's called shopping for what you don't want. You don't want that do you? We didn't think so. If you believe you are not smart with money, then you will act and continue to think in a way that supports that belief. Likewise, if you believe and practice thinking that you are savvy with money, you will prove yourself right about it over and over again. What we verbalize - and even what we just think in our minds - will continue to be true because we don't want to make ourselves wrong. The human mind will do all it can to move us toward what we truly, 100% believe to be true; it's basic quantum physics. As soon as we say something, the universe conspires in our favor to make it true for us. Of course, this requires consistent action. The string of creating any result goes like this: ideas create emotions, emotions create actions and actions create results. Each of those elements must be managed carefully and consistently in your world if you are going to create the results you would LOVE!

> "Right now you are looking at the results of your past creations. And right now how you feel is creating your future."
> – Odille Rault, "Beyond the Magic Pill"

Starting a business is the best personal development course you could possibly take - if you're up for it and totally committed to it, that is. When you start a business, you are instantly confronted with all of your personal and professional baggage. You'll learn a lot about yourself, and you'll probably want to give up at times, but those areas that are triggering you are probably what's stopping you in all areas of your life, so you may as well plow through them.

We all have had experiences in our lives that we're not proud of, or wish we could change. I'm pretty sure I've had more than my share. I've carried around a story of not being good enough for a good chunk of my life, and in some ways, that has helped me to be successful, and in others, it has caused a lot of pain. There are very strong "away values" tied to the "I'm not good enough" story. I learned I wasn't good enough to be a cheerleader in high school, even though all my friends were. I learned I wasn't "good enough" for my mom when she found out I was pregnant at eighteen years old. I learned I wasn't "good enough" when my marriage failed. The good news, for me and for you, is that there's a flip side to this. The "toward value" that I've embraced is my "whatever it takes" attitude. It's what keeps me up until 3 a.m. writing a book. It's what got me through my son's toddler years, when I worked as a waitress from 5 a.m. to 8 a.m. at the Holiday Inn, took my son to daycare, worked my 9-to-5 temp job, then went to school from 6 p.m. until 10 p.m. at night. It's what got me to invest in my first flip, my first rental, and my first apartment building. You see, we can always write our own stories. It's up to you to decide. I've learned to do it, to live it and to "flip" my story around, and so can you!

Let's take a look at how a little personal development work improved Rebecca's life.

Retired Rebecca

When I used to work long flights, like New York to Paris, we would often have a lot of downtime. I liked to listen to audio recordings a lot, and often chose Tony Robbins and Zig Ziglar as my mentors. I think I liked those so much because my husband always listened to them in the car whenever we went for long drives. I liked their key messages, and they reminded me of my husband on those long flights.

Then after I retired, I joined a women's group in my community dedicated to giving back. We ran auctions for charities and held a community dinner for senior citizens once a week. Over this time period, I worked hard as a volunteer and organizer, and I always found it to be well worth it.

It is interesting, though. I had always read that to give and contribute value to another's life was a way to generate material wealth. Yet I was so rich in giving and looking constantly for opportunities to give, that my bank account stayed at a modest level. I could only ever give my time, my energy and my skills; I rarely found myself in a position where I could make financial contributions.

It was right after I signed up for the real estate investing seminar that something hit me. I wanted to learn how to create wealth so that I could give more money, which was in line with my core values. It was time to increase my earnings so that I could reclaim some of my time that I had been donating to my women's group. Placing a value on my time and energy like that made me realize just how little I had valued myself in the past. It took a boost of belief in myself and a dose of raised self-esteem to firmly step into the new pattern I was going to create – and it felt great!

The process of transitioning into being a business owner, or a savvy investor, or to being financially independent, requires that you do some personal development work. Otherwise, you're likely to stay stuck in patterns and beliefs that will cause everything you've worked for to slip through your fingers. There is luck, and there is skill. Doing the personal development work to dive a little deeper into your mindset is like laying the groundwork for a solid foundation. And, since your mindset is your reality, when you get it into shape, you literally shift from a "reality by default" to a "reality of your choosing."

D. What Is Your Identity?

A great next step for you is to consider what your true identity is. The beauty of this piece is that at any given moment you have the ability to decide what it is. A great exercise is to write out your ideal version of you. There's nobody better to map out your character traits, values and stakes in the ground than you. When you carefully create the picture of the ideal version of you, you can begin practicing it in your imagination. That is the place where it becomes true first, before you'll ever realize it in the real world. When you're ready to become an investor in real estate and a successful, professional game-changer in the world, let your imagination take you there in every detail. Just write it down and don't stop until every time you read your words, you get inspired, excited and can say, "YES, That's me!"

CHECK UP FROM THE NECK UP
What are the last five books you read?
1.
2.
3.
4.
5.

LIST OF RESOURCES TO EXPAND YOUR THINKING – Margaret's Personal Top Five MUST READ (or listen to) List
What are the last five books you read?
1. Think and Grow Rich by Napoleon Hill
2. The Compound Effect by Darren Hardy
3. Essentialism: The Disciplined Pursuit of Less by Greg McKeown
4. The Science of Getting Rich by Wallace D. Wattles
5. The Four Agreements by Don Miguel Ruiz

When I truly took on the identity of real estate investor and when I committed to that identity, along with so many other empowering characteristics that were important to me, I could feel it with all my senses. My new identity changed my behavior. This was the birth of the total certainty that carried me to taking immediate action, to finding the funding for and ultimately investing again and again in real estate as I built my growing real estate portfolio.

One other powerful tool you'll want to use as you further define your "ideal" version of you is what I refer to as the power of contrast. Make a list of everyone who has ever inspired you. Then, seek out others who might inspire you in some way. Is it Oprah, Richard Branson, Steve Jobs? You decide. Then, research how they lived, their adventures, their traits, rituals, lifestyle choices and more. You may even find inspiration in celebrity movie characters. Maybe you find inspiration from some aspect of Miranda in The Devil Wears Prada, or from a book where a woman leaves her full-time job and builds a real estate enterprise. Take the time to find your own inspirations. Life will constantly throw you little peeks at inspirations that will light you up inside and drive you forward. In my life I've been inspired by Tony Robbins, Bill Hybels and Brené Brown. Why? I've seen something in each of them and the mark they've made in the world that I'd love to make in my own way. When I think of the areas of their lives that inspire me, I'm able to adopt those positive and powerful traits into my own identity and behavior and become a stronger, more powerful and capable version of me.

Live as If...

Something becomes true as soon as it's true in your mind. I like the phrase, "live as if." Not "fake it 'til you make it," but "live as if." If you were living as if you were a writer, where would you spend your time? How would you dress? Where would you live? What would you stop or start doing in your daily life? What does your house look like? Who are you associating with? If you're a writer, then are your top five people that you're associating with supporting and promoting your aspirations? Are they making you feel good about being a writer? Are they challenging you to be writing more or in a different way? Are they sharing ideas, systems and challenges that pull you up to the next level and raise your game?

Here's a test: If someone took a picture of you in your home and was going to post it on the front cover of People magazine, would you be proud of your physical appearance? Would you be proud of the way your house looks today—your kitchen, your bathroom, your closet? Is your laundry in the basket or eighteen inches away from the basket? These are habits and standards that show up in every area of your life; what shows up on the outside is a direct reflection of what is going on inside. We will spend more time later in the book with some exercises to turn your "live as if" into a new reality for your life—one where you are proud of how you're living, with your newly raised standards.

I ran a seminar once where a participant shared an inspiring story. I had done an exercise where I asked if people were really embracing their identity. I was talking about how the world will show up differently depending on how you show up and also WHO you show up as. Some people don't want to invest in real estate because they think they lack what it takes. In this one case, this person believed she was missing the "investor gene," or that her investing abilities somehow got shortchanged.

She said, "I just can't see myself as an investor, because I've always been a teacher!" There were all kinds of people in the seminar; we had a fireman, a university professor and many others. They all had identities they were carrying with them and some of them had a really hard time coming up with a new identity beyond, "I'm only a teacher and have always been one. I just want to make more money." It's true that if your primary drive to becoming an investor is to make more money, then you will experience hesitation and disbelief and you will struggle to step into your potential. You have to see yourself as an investor – a.k.a., someone who invests in something to then create more value and then provide more value for others in the world. It doesn't mean that's the only thing you do, but make sure that identity is rock solid.

The woman at the seminar came back the next day and said, "I'm shocked. I am shifting!" For the first time, she had told somebody that she was an investor. She had gone back to work for a few hours before returning to my seminar, and had engaged in a conversation with the janitor, "Yes, I was at a seminar and I'm a real estate investor," the participant told the janitor. She told us that she had said it in a really uncomfortable way, as it was the first time the words had come out of her mouth – as her true identity. More than that, she didn't share the message to brag or convince anyone. She wasn't sharing it to sell either. She was just sharing a truth – and as she said, "It felt great to live as if!"

The janitor replied telling her that he had $50,000 of his own that he was hoping to invest and he wanted to talk to her about it. All of a sudden the janitor thought our participant must know what she's doing! And guess what, another key lesson to learn is that you have all you need today to be a successful real estate investor, because you can always reach out to a team of the right advisors who provide excellent mentorship and coaching. This is advice we can all glean from Henry Ford who had a series of red buttons on his desk. He noted that he could reach out to get all the answers he needed just by knowing who to ask. His advisors were on the other end of those red buttons. Get the idea?

What is it that you identify with now and is that in conflict with the direction you want to go? Let's say you identify with being a mom, or maybe you identify with being a corporate person, or a teacher. Whatever your identity is, you want to move forward and become a real estate investor. You're moving toward a value— your identity as a real estate investor. Where might there be a conflict?

You might have a story about what it means to be a real estate investor, and this often ties in with money beliefs, too. If you think that rich people are bad, self-ish, greedy or whatever their stories are, there might be some pain associated with moving toward that. Or, maybe you've never learned how to generate value and revenue in your life. A great lesson that I've learned from one of my mentors, Tony Robbins, is that, "The past doesn't equal the future!" Today is a clean slate, so go after it as the brilliant and resourceful woman you are. The universe will meet you on the road to your success. Can you feel that? It's your new identity forming as we speak!

Isn't it time to take full ownership of the lifestyle and business you really love and deserve? Isn't it time to start valuing yourself? And not because you need a big pile of

---

Write Your I AM Statements HERE....

---

money in the bank or because it's already there. Decide right now that your success is not measured by your bank account. It's simply a decision to make successful choices, to access successful guidance and mentors and to take massive action in the direction of your dreams without letting anything hold you back.

If you're still feeling like becoming a full-time real estate investor will somehow detract from your identity as a mom, or as a wife (I mean, what if you start making more than your spouse - right?), you're not alone. That's a common issue that women sometimes have, even though it sounds crazy to people who aren't in that situation. The relationship dynamic can change greatly if suddenly you're making more money than your spouse. Recent labor statistics show that women now represent nearly half of the U.S. labor force—and that in 38 percent of American marriages, the woman out-earns her husband; that's a significant increase from 1987, when less than 25 percent of women were the primary earners in their families.

When you do your personal development work, you will have the opportunity to take a close look at your rules. If your rules state that your definition of success is earning as much as, but not more than your spouse, you'll set your "money thermostat" too low and then position yourself to sabotage your success along the way – no matter how well things are going in building your investment business. It is through exploring your thoughts and rules and asking these questions that you'll start taking an active role in choosing the path most in line with your highest values. This is where you truly begin to create the life you love.

What are the habits or rules you have adopted in your life about money, about what success means to you, or about what your earnings should be as they relate to your spouse? Feel free to explore this deeply, and write them below, because rules can be changed. This is a great time to see what rules you have that make you feel like a failure, even if you are successful.

Example: My habit is believing that to be successful you must have $1 million in the bank at all times in liquid cash.

The above habit is a surefire way to feel like a failure. It will also teach you to keep an enormous amount of money out of your investments and therefore not working for you. Also, it tells you that you can't be successful until you've reached that goal and that just isn't true! Set benchmarks and rules that empower you, not the opposite.

HABITS AND RULES
THAT ARE KEEPING YOU BROKE

My habit? I can recite it verbatim because I have it written on an index card that's taped to my bathroom mirror: "MONEY FLOWS FREELY AND EASILY."

Now, your turn.

NEW HABIT

E. The Way You Do Anything Is the Way You Do Everything

Along your personal development journey, regardless of what books you read or what courses you take, you will inevitably be faced with yourself – the good, the bad, and the ugly. You will be invited at some point to take stock of how you live. And you will doubtless read and hear the old adage, "The way you do anything is the way you do everything."

If you leave things messy and undone in your car, then things are probably also messy and undone in your house, in your closet, in your business, in your finances, and in your relationships – oh and worst place of all – IN YOUR HEAD!

The lack of initiative that a particular person demonstrates in reaching any meaningful goal in their life reveals their overall weakness towards creating results in every other area of their life.

When Cathy began working with Maggie, one of the early sessions was exactly about helping Cathy to see where she had been consistent and inconsistent in how she did things in her life.

Corporate Cathy

Maggie and I met by Skype for our one-on-one session, once a week on a Wednesday evening. We had only had three sessions so far, and I was really enjoying them. I appreciated Maggie's easy and pleasant way of asking great questions that helped guide me to each little breakthrough – sometimes just in my own awareness. In today's session, we talked about identity.

"Okay Cathy, I want to walk you through an exercise. Do you have your pen and paper handy?"

I nodded and held it up to the screen to show her, "And my glass of wine, too!"

Maggie laughed. I appreciated that it was the evening and she never criticized me if I wanted to have a glass of wine during the session. She was in favor of most self-care activities, and not a radical anti-sugar and alcohol person. I loved that about her as well, I guess, her "realness."

"Great. So, let's first make a list of areas in your life you want to improve. Don't hold back. Say them out loud while you're writing them too, so I can hear."

I thought about it for a minute, then began to write. "I want to kick the Starbucks habit. I stop at Starbucks every time I run errands."

"Good," Maggie said. "What else?"

I looked at my glass of wine. I sure did love my evening glass of wine, but it was true, I was beginning to gain weight. I could feel it – a pair of my jeans wasn't fitting as well anymore too. "Okay, and I will stop buying three bottles of wine a week."

Maggie asked gently, "Is that realistic?" She knew how much I loved my wine.

"Okay, I will only buy one bottle of wine a week." I looked at Maggie on the screen, and she nodded with a smile.

"How much will this save you, Cathy?"

I added up the money I was spending on Starbucks and wine. I was amazed. "$65 a week!" I said, surprised.

Maggie laughed, "A lot, isn't it? Now, where could you redirect that money so that you can use your time more wisely?"

I thought about it, chewing on the end of my pen. "I suppose I could use help with cleaning the house.

It's not something I enjoy, and I don't like spending my time doing it."

"Okay, what would that look like?"

"Well, for $65 a week I could have a cleaning person come in and do the house once a week."

Maggie asked, "And what would that do for you, especially? Besides giving you a clean house. How would you spend the time you might otherwise spend cleaning?"

"Maybe I will join an association. I saw a flyer for the Real Estate Investor's Association – maybe I can start there?"

Maggie nodded. "That might be an excellent starting place, considering your goals we went over last week. Why not?"

I felt excited at the prospect of joining the association, and of not having to clean my house. For the first time since I hatched the seeds of my plan, I felt hope that I was able to make the changes I knew I needed to make. I was on my way to creating my life.

If Cathy can do it, you can too. Take a moment and do the following exercise and discover what small shifts you can make to help you start stepping into the life you want to create.

Exercise: *Look at the area of your life where you need the most improvement. Whatever is at the root cause of that area is probably carried over in all areas of your life. Use this exercise to take a careful inventory of each life area. Look at the basics first: health, relationships, finances, family, business/career, time, fun/adventure, contribution, spiritual, emotional, lifelong learning.*

What is one frustration you have in each area?

What is something you can start and something you can stop to make an improvement in this area of your life?

Why MUST you make this change?
[This is called getting leverage.]

Lastly, what are the steps to creating each change and then, when will you begin by taking the first step and when will you have achieved your shift in each area? [suggestion: START NOW!]

Decision-Making

We live and die by the decisions we make, unless of course you are one of those people who don't make any decisions, which leaves your business at a standstill. Which in itself is a decision—it is a decision to not make decisions. If you don't make decisions in your business you are going to get stuck.

> *"Consider this – the opposite of decision-making is procrastination...and procrastination is the prime cause of failure!"*
> **– Margaret Wright**

I have a sign that says, "I got where I am today by making decisions."

It doesn't matter which decision you make. If you make one decision over the other, at least you did something that's going to move you forward into action. It might end up being the wrong decision, but you can go back, course correct, and make that decision right in some way. If you start to trust yourself that when you make the decision you can always make it right, it makes the decision-making process less scary.

Decision saboteurs to watch out for:
- Not making a decision in the first place.
- Not following through with your decisions.
- Decision flip-flopping, going back and forth between different decisions.
- Not fully committing to your decision – emotionally, and with an action plan.
- Letting someone else influence you to make a decision that isn't what you want or doesn't allow you to go after your dream.
- Making a decision solely based on money.

- *Only* making decisions from your gut.
- Making a decision before you have all the information.
- Making a decision based on what other people will think of you.

Life doesn't put a limit on the number of decisions you make, but you put a limit on your life by not making decisions. When you have to make a hard decision, flip a coin. Why? Because when the coin is in the air you suddenly know what you're hoping for.

EXERCISE: MAKE GREAT BUSINESS DECISIONS Here is my process for making great business decisions. Ask yourself these questions:
What is the potential ROI (return on investment)?
What are the business benefits?
What are the life benefits?
Am I committed to the outcome?
Am I committed to the follow-through?
Do I feel it in my gut that this is the right decision?

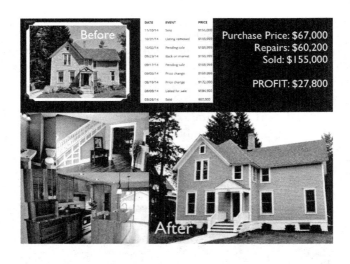

SECTION 2

SPACE

A. You Dictate Your Environment

It's interesting to examine the influence our outside environment has on us. This is beyond the age-old nature versus nurture question; it's already been scientifically proven that 40% of our genetic expression is due to influence. Do you think your surroundings might have an impact on your success as well? Take a look around you right now. The scary thing is, you're probably so used to your peripheral space that you're oblivious.

> "If you make sure that your environment supports your dreams, achieving your dreams becomes radically easier. Whatever you are surrounded by all day influences you more than you think."
> **– Author Unknown**

Sorry, ladies it's the truth. I'm going to give you a loving reality check and some easy tips to make sure your outside world is positively influencing your inside world. This is another area that you must evaluate and act on if you're going to own it.

Let's start with your morning wake up routine. What's the first thing you see? Do you pick up your phone and check email or Facebook? What's on your nightstand – sleeping pills, mindless fiction or books about living on purpose? Do you own that space?

When I wake up, I look at a picture of the loves of my life, my children, and the following quote from Louise Hay, "My day begins and ends with gratitude and joy."

Now, it might seem like a very subtle difference between reading a positive and affirming quote and seeing the cover of *Fifty Shades of Grey*. Don't get me wrong; I don't blame you for appreciating the rock hard body of a millionaire, but who wants that kind of distraction when on a mission to OWN IT? I'm far more inclined to BE the millionaire with a rock hard body than to want to read about one.

The next thing I see is my vision board, and guess what? There's a rock hard body there too. So what's the difference? Intention and attention. A seedy romance novel is an escape from reality. A vision board is a picture of the life you desire and are actually pursuing and taking steps toward every day.

Next, we're going to create a new habit, a daily habit of guaranteed success. Who doesn't want to start their day with a win? Make your bed!

There was a great speech given by a Navy Seal at a graduation ceremony. His best piece of advice was to make your bed every day. He goes so far as to say, "If you want to change the world, start off by making your bed. If you make your bed every morning, you will have accomplished the first task of the day. It will give you a sense of pride and it will encourage you to do another task and another and another and by the end of the day, that one task completed will have turned into many tasks completed."

Let's take a look at the psychology of going to bed in a disheveled heap of blankets and pillows. Now the first "task" that you should have completed when the sun first came up is still sitting there lingering, mocking you, the last reminder of what was not done no matter how productive the day may have been. You failed to accomplish the simple first task.

Contrast this to the feeling of walking into your sleep space, your retreat, your haven, your small slice of heaven to lay your head down before you slumber. Rather than yanking and pulling on crumpled, wrinkled sheets, you gracefully stretch your body across the welcoming sleep space. You spritz a little lavender sheet spray, sip sparkling water out of a crystal goblet because you deserve nothing but the best—and there's evidence surrounding you to remind you of that fact. You own it, girl.

Go ahead and spare yourself. Cut out the garbage of watching the news, reading the paper, the Yahoo newsfeed, CNN - all well known to be constantly negative news. Replace all those soul-sucking sources with books (audio or written), quotes, pictures, and visions that inspire you. You are what you eat, and your mind is consuming everything your eyes and ears are taking in. Guard it. Filter in. Own it. Take a close look around you. The clothes on your body, the sheets on your bed, the carpet under your feet. Is there evidence of your fabulous life?

Today, make a list of ten things you don't absolutely love and purge them from your life. Maybe it's a pair of pants that don't fit quite right or that coffee mug your ex gave you for your drive to the office. Mix it up. Start to examine your life. When you own it, you get to choose what you love, who you love, what makes you smile. Have more of this every day. Do what you want, where you want and with whom you want. It takes a deliberate focused effort to eliminate the garbage and step into the life you love and deserve to have.

Let's take a look at how Tara benefited from sprucing up her environment, before you try it yourself with an exercise.

Teacher Tara

Although I had already signed up for the course, several friends, all of whom had strong opinions on how to spend my money, still tried to talk me out of it. My girlfriends— who prefer to spend money on shoes and handbags—couldn't believe I was ready to drop thousands of dollars down so willingly for an online course. I ignored them. Something told me this was a real investment; I just couldn't see exactly how it would play out yet.

After the values exercise, we were guided to do a vision board. I dove headfirst into this activity, and loved every minute of it. I didn't quite get the connection between this work and the actual wealth principles the course promised, but I trusted the facilitator, and the process.

I found a stack of magazines, mostly of homes and décor, some travel, bought a small mounted canvas and sat down one afternoon to create my vision board. I put on some of my favorite music, and worked in the bright afternoon sunlight as it hit my kitchen table, one of my favorite places to work in the condo.

I let myself envision with reckless abandon. There were pictures of gorgeous kitchens, living rooms, bedrooms; all were quite minimal in design, but featured elegant fabrics and prints. I cut up pictures of couples and scattered them throughout the collage, daydreaming about my future partner and what he might look like (tall, dark and handsome) and what he might do for a living (entrepreneur – so we can spend our summers traveling together). The more I let my mind daydream freely, the more images I found to support my dreams.

I included several book titles, to represent the library I hope my future home will have. I have always been an avid reader, and I envisioned a library with floor to ceiling bookshelves, featuring all of the classics of literature and an extensive reference section.

I was so enchanted with creating my vision board that I barely noticed the passage of time. It wasn't until the light changed from bright afternoon light to the early evening light that I realized how late it was. I finished my collage, and hung it up that evening. I stood in my room, admiring it for a long time.

The last part of the course had been a brief discussion on creating a positive space in general. I understood the importance of this, for the most part, although when the facilitator instructed us to "make our bed" each morning as a profound tool for discipline and development, I laughed out loud. My mom always used to tell me to make my bed. And of course, my mother kept an impeccable home. She was a stay-at-home mom, it was supposed to be that way. I was single and lived alone. Who cared whether or not I made my bed?

I made it anyway, even though it was 8 p.m. that night. I made it, then left the room. I went out, did a few things, and when I finally went to bed at midnight, I could not deny that I was happy to climb into a bed that was ready for me. It felt energetically ready for a new night's sleep, all memory of the previous night's sleep having been swept away in the simple act of pulling up bedsheets and smoothing out the duvet. Hmmm, I could get used to this.

I decided to make my bed each morning, and spend a few moments looking at my vision board. What the heck, I thought, it couldn't hurt, right?

Rebecca also decided to take action on clearing her space to set up her ideal environment. Here is what she experienced.

Retired Rebecca

I went to the seminar on my own. I wasn't surprised that my husband had no interest, and I didn't necessarily care. I still wasn't even sure why I was going, except for a nagging curiosity. I had a feeling there was something for me there, I just didn't know what yet.

I had never been particularly drawn to money and numbers, and I thought real estate was for the big players. So, the idea of going to a seminar on how to invest in real estate was a little off topic for me. Still, I was desperate to come up with a plan to afford retirement, and soon. I'd had enough of my job. I had time but not a lot of money, and without the money, I felt like I was wasting my time.

The first part of the seminar was casual and seemed to be about topics that didn't connect. For instance, we were told to go home that night and de-clutter, first thing. I wasn't sure what de-cluttering had to do with making money in real estate, but I trusted the facilitator so much that I did it.

When I went home, I did a complete purge of my closet, head to toe. I threw out bell-bottoms I had worn in the '70s and clothes that no longer fit. I got rid of papers that we no longer needed to store (old magazines, receipts and bills from ten years ago). I enjoyed purging, and wondered why I didn't do it more often. As I freed up more space in my closet, I could feel more space in my mind free up. "Huh," I thought to myself, "Maybe this is why they have us do this?" I could feel the freedom to allow new ideas to come to me in the space that had been created by de-cluttering.

PURGE EXERCISE
Now, it's your turn to de-clutter. Go through your closets, your cabinets, your drawers to rid yourself of anything that is no longer serving you. Ask yourself about each item: Do I absolutely love it? Would I pay to own it today? Have I used/worn it in the past 12 months? If you answer no to ANY of these, or if in doubt... throw it out.

Purchase Price: $55,777
Repairs: $50,000
Sold: $140,000

PROFIT: $50,000

Purchase Price: $59,000
Repairs: $59,500
Sold: $157,000

PROFIT: $38,500

Live the image of who you want to become.
- Dress
- Schedule your time
- Declutter
- Priorities

SECTION 3

TIME

Everybody has the same amount of time. Do you want more time? Stop watching reality television and the news, and ration your time on social media.

Most people don't have any idea where they're spending their time. Step back and take an assessment of where you spend yours. For instance, what did you accomplish in the last fifteen minutes? The last hour? The last day? The last week? Was it intentional or was it reactive? Was it by default or did you plan it? Success leaves clues. Look at someone's car: if it is immaculate and kept in pristine condition, that says something about them. Look at their body: are they someone who gets up at 5 a.m. and goes to the gym, or are they someone who gets up at 9 a.m. and goes to Starbucks? You can tell by looking at someone.

It's a real eye-opener, isn't it? Once you have an idea of this particular truth of where you are, you can own that truth and start to identify where you're not okay with what reality looks like, when it comes to your time, in the present moment. Only then can you say, "What would I really like to do? Where would I like to spend my time?" If your family is a priority and you spend one hour with them at dinner three times a week, then they're not really a priority are they? Where you spend your time should reflect your priorities and what's important to you.

We experience pain points when we don't use our time in a way that aligns with our true values. We know we don't want more of one thing, while we do want more of another. We close the gap when we choose to spend time in favor of what we do want.

Figure out what your time is worth, what you want your income to be and how much time you want to be working. Let's look at those numbers backwards. First, how many hours do you want to be working? Let's say you want to work 10 hours a week. That might sound crazy now, but I assure you, when you OWN IT, that might be a busy week. If you want to make $100k per year, working 10 hours per week for 52 weeks, you value your time at $192/hour. That's more than reasonable as a beginner real estate investor, and certainly a good goal to start with. Are you doing something else that's worth that much? If not, how do you make yourself more valuable? Could it be by educating yourself to be a savvy investor, by starting a new business, so that the return you get for your time is what you know your time is worth?

Ask yourself this—is what you're currently doing ever going to get you there? If you're a school teacher and you're making $45,000 a year but you want to be making $1 million a year, you have to stop just being a school teacher. It doesn't mean you have to stop being a teacher, but without making a change, you will keep getting what you've gotten, which is the result of trading a lot of your time for not a lot of money.

Even if you're flipping houses and you're somebody who wants to get in, get dirty and do the work, then your time is limited by what you can do yourself. When you learn to delegate, then you realize, "Hey, instead of doing one house at a time, I can do two houses at a time." It's worth paying somebody $25 an hour, or even $50 an hour to take on the responsibilities that you used to do. Even though you might be giving up a little bit of the profit, what's the return on your time and energy?

I can be flipping ten houses per quarter, making $25,000 each without having to show up to the job. I would gladly pay somebody $100,000 a year to be the project manager of that business. If that means I'm making $900,000 per year instead of $1 million a year, then for me, that's a good reallocation of my time, energy, and resources.

My checklist of the biggest timewasters are social media, television, and not working off of a plan. Any time that you spend in reaction is a waste of time. Any time that's not planned and allocated proactively is potentially a waste of time.

If there's no value whatsoever in doing it, it's a waste of time. The best example is watching television. Television is an absolute no-brainer. There is no good that's going to come from watching hours of made up stories about fake people for hours every night. There's no improvement to your life that's going to come from watching the Kardashians doing whatever the hell the Kardashians do.

There are things that you could be doing with your time that are much more valuable. If you spend all day

Saturday doing the dishes, doing the laundry and scrubbing your toilets, then you're never going to move out of the mindset of "it's my responsibility to do that because that's what my time is worth." That's the value of your contribution to this world right now. This is really the next level of time management, when you stop doing things that are a complete waste of time, and you delegate things that are necessary.

Consider, what is your highest value? If it's earning passive income via real estate, get yourself educated. There's a huge return on your education, so invest your time in something that's going to get you a return. That's really what it is all about. Are you investing your time in something that will give you a return? If so, what is that return? Are you measuring it?

The return you might get on doing your dishes is that you're going to sleep better. You're going to feel good that your kitchen is clean, but that's fleeting. You could invest a half hour a day, and in a year you could speak Spanish. Most people will tell you, "I have no time, I have no time, I have no time," meanwhile they've invested three hours a week in watching their favorite Netflix original. After a year, what do they have? Nothing. There's a misconception about how much time it will take to get a result, and it's because they're not mapping it out properly. They're not really being deliberate with it. They're not taking control of their time. Committed action is what is required.

Rebecca understood the value right away in investing in her education. As soon as the free one-day seminar she took had wrapped for the day, she decided to enroll in a full two-day immersion seminar. She had a strong feeling in her heart that this investment would yield big rewards for her, and she signed up then and there. She knew if she asked her husband or friends first, they would have talked her out of it.

Retired Rebecca

After the first seminar, which was free, I was sold. I could see the value so clearly. I had not invested in myself, or my education, in what felt like forever. In fact, I had not invested in my own education, on a formal level, since college. To really decide to invest in myself by taking a course that would educate and empower me was a pivotal decision to make. I felt so proud of what I was role-modeling to my daughters. I didn't worry a minute about paying for the course, I just knew I had to take it.

A. No Extra Time

There's a catchphrase I love called NET – No Extra Time. When we talk about NET, we're talking about the "no extra time" it takes to do things that will drastically improve the quality of your life. It's amazing what you can catch in your NET every day. Reading books is one of my favorites; I regularly listen to one or two Audible books per week. People will often say, "I don't have any time to read books," but is that really true?

Think about when you drive your kids to school in the morning, or for us FlipChicks, when we're driving to meet a contractor. The drive might be only ten minutes, but you can listen to an audio book for that ten minutes. If you have enough ten-, twenty-, and thirty-minute increments of time in the car, you can easily listen to one audio book per week. That alone brings great value to your life, whether it's an audio book on time management, spirituality, or real estate. Again, *Fifty Shades of Grey* doesn't count!

There are people who have closed gaps in their lives that are the same gaps you're trying to close in your life—and many of them have written books about it. It would be foolish to miss out on the opportunity to take advantage of the lessons learned by people who have gone before us, who have gotten to the place where we want to be. For us to spend ten minutes a day toward closing that gap is not invasive. It's ten minutes of pressing play and listening while you're driving, doing the dishes or putting on your mascara.

I have had to make choices that were sometimes a little difficult, but had to be done in order to reach my goals. For one, I had to stop hanging out with my neighbors. They came over every single night. At first, I thought, "Oh, this is cool. I love having a social life," and then three hours would go by and we had done nothing but drink wine. Most of the time I felt like I was coaching them! If I wasn't the one talking, the conversation turned into talking about someone's kids, somebody's wife, somebody's this and somebody's that, and the life just got sucked out of me.

It's not wrong to have some down time, but do it in a directed way. If you want to see what's happening on social media, set the timer and allow yourself ten minutes to be on it. It's your schedule, your life - just take control of it.

Wasting time is really a habit. We also often waste time because we are likely avoiding something or procrastinating. Sometimes you may think, "I just need a break." Well take a break, but make it a good one. Going for a walk for fifteen minutes is far more valuable than spending that fifteen minutes on social media.

Recognize the why. What were you doing that all of a sudden you found yourself on Facebook for an hour? Were you overwhelmed because work got too hard? Were you frustrated that you didn't feel like you were making progress? Were you just tired?

People will spend hours every night watching television. When you think about what you really want, or even something on your bucket list, like learning a new language, you can do it in ten minutes a day. That's it. You want to run a marathon, then it's just a scheduled and structured number of hours per week of running. You can start to train as a runner in as little as twenty minutes a day, and if you can do that, you can run a marathon. There is a schedule, and there are steps that get you there... no different than your wealth goals.

I love challenging people. When somebody tells me what their excuses are, I remind them that excuses are just that, excuses. Be honest with yourself that you are making excuses. Then challenge yourself. Make yourself do something that will improve your life.

That's the only way you can grow.

Give Up the No Time Excuse - You have the time.

NET time - No Extra Time to do these things. Make a list of things you think you have "NET" to do each week, and determine times you can do these in small increments. Think driving to pick up kids, doing the dishes, cleaning, laundry, or any other incremental times where you might listen to an audio book or learn a language. Of course, once you delegate many of these tasks, your NET might be driving to yoga, taking a long hot bath, or going for a run.

Exercise: Look at how much time you spend on social media in a day. What if you spent that time doing something else? What if you just went on a social media diet for a week, how much could you get done?

BONUS: Cut out the mind trash.

• No Facebook/Twitter/Pinterest... for a week

• Reality TV

• Gossip

• Reactive Texting

• Tinder

• Energy or Time Vampires

• Online Shopping

None of these things are wrong – just do it in a directed way. Set the timer, allow yourself ten minutes to do it. You will be amazed how, when you give yourself ten minutes to find the replacement filter for your air purifier, that it really only took you six minutes, including checkout. So, why did last time take forty-five minutes of "browsing" on Amazon, to end up with three items you didn't have on your list when you logged in? Hmmm? Not only will being deliberate save you time, it will save you money and space in your closets.

B. Every Woman Needs a Wife

We all have spent some time doing things we *have to* do in life. Not every "to do" on our list is going to be fun or enjoyable, that's for sure. We're all bound to have tasks we hate. To that we say, delegate!

Let's look at how Cathy started to delegate, after that coaching session she had with Maggie.

Corporate Cathy

After my third coaching session with Maggie, I really felt fired up. She gave me homework – to make a list of what I hate. Well, I thought hate was a harsh word, but WOW… look at my list:

- Picking up my dry cleaning
- Grocery shopping
- Filling up my gas tank
- Shopping for birthday gifts
- Taking the dog to the groomers
- Picking up the dog poop
- "Spring cleaning" the garage

The next mission was to delegate what I hate. Maggie suggested the sooner the better, so that same afternoon I set aside two hours to find someone who loves these dreaded tasks. My mind was blown as I scoured the Internet and found websites like Care.com, Taskrabbit, and of course old standbys like Craigslist and Monster.com.

Despite seeing these sites, I began by posting on Facebook, "I need a wife!" That got a lot of curious comments. I listed the tasks I was looking to "outsource" and I was shocked to find that within an hour I had private messages from half a dozen friends and friends of friends who were interested and would LOVE (who in their right mind would love these dreaded tasks?!) to talk about helping me.

I not only found a wife, I found three wives. A doggy wife, a house wife and an errands wife. It's been two weeks since that session, and my house hasn't been cleaner, my dog hasn't been happier, and my "to do" list is "to DONE."

Create a "Delegate What You Hate" List

Do you want to experience the relief Cathy felt? First, make a list of things that you hate. What do you most dislike doing? You don't like to do dishes. You hate ironing. The list goes on. If you don't absolutely love it, you shouldn't have to do it. There's no reason to.

There are also things you may hate doing, but you love the result, and you can't delegate it. For example, you can't reasonably delegate brushing your teeth or working out. I haven't found a way to delegate brushing my teeth, but it's pretty easy to find a personal trainer to come to your house.

If your "why" is strong enough, the "how to" will always show up. You want to look good or have a strong body. You want a clean house. You want a healthy relationship... so you do the necessary work to ensure these things happen.

What about errands? Getting the groceries, paying the bills, all the logistical things that you need to do to get you through the day. How much of these can you realistically delegate? Personal assistants can pick up groceries and dry cleaning. An excellent personal assistant can manage your bills or other clerical tasks.

I have delegated all kinds of tasks away. At first it was all the things I didn't like doing. In the beginning, there was a little voice in my head that would whisper, "Margaret, the dishes aren't done. You're the mom, it's your job to make sure the dishes are done. Go do your dishes or you're a bad mom... a bad wife... a bad woman." Well, no, I shouldn't be doing the dishes. Somebody else should be doing the dishes, because I hate doing the dishes. It's hard to imagine a time when I didn't have the help I enjoy now, but there was a time I didn't. As silly as it seems, having someone to wash those damn dishes became a strong motivation for me. I knew if I wanted it bad enough and worked toward my goal, then I would have enough money so I could pay somebody to do the dishes.

The other thing that is really helpful to know is that the people who work for us in our homes love coming to work for us. They love that they can have their kids in school during the day, come to our home and take care of things while they're in school, and still get to be full-time moms.

Find someone who loves doing the tasks you hate, and delegate. You are doing someone a favor by giving them a job, and you are raising the value on your own time to reflect what your time is truly worth.

Exercise: What are your time wasters?

REALITY CHECK Where do you spend your time? [use a timetable]

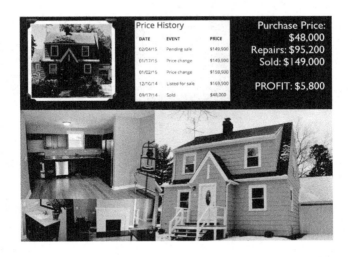

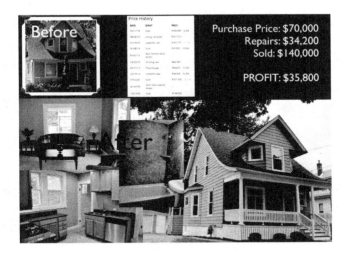

MONEY

"MONEY IS..." EXERCISE

Before you read this chapter, take a moment and do this simple exercise. Just write down "Money is..." and for the next three minutes, write all the words that come to your mind in response to these words.

Power   Freedom   Fun!

Choices   Energy

Opportunities   Wealth

Confidence   Abundance

Shopping   Nice things

Quality   Easy

Joy!   Giving   Exchange

Let's see what Tara, Cathy and Rebecca wrote.

Teacher Tara: Money is... smart, opportunity, nice things, easy

Corporate Cathy: Money is... freedom, health, time, sharing

Retired Rebecca: Money is... giving, adventure, caring, helping out

Now, put your answers away and read the chapter. At the end of the whole section, try this exercise again. Let us know what you find out!

A. Why Women Are Better at Investing Than Men

I'm going to make a statement that might sound a bit bold. Women are better at investing than men. Yes, I believe it. Men are more interested in getting results, which makes them riskier investors. As women, we have more to protect. Imagine, if you're a mom and you're looking for security, you're less likely to take unnecessary risks. We tend to be more calculated with our investing.

As women, we're more emotionally invested in the result, so we put more time and energy into it. In fact, it might be easier to walk away. If things are not going well, we're more inclined to take a step back and reevaluate instead of just pushing through. As opposed to a hunting mindset - "We're going for it!" - we're more of the gathering mindset.

This is why compounding works for women. Women generally have more patience than men; they have patience to nurture and see something grow. Growing an investment portfolio is like raising a child, or growing a family. If you think about it in terms of raising a kid, for example, a baby starts out and they need their diaper changed. Women have the patience to do that over and over and over, without getting frustrated. Whereas, a man might look at the diaper after 100 times and say, "Why am I doing this? This isn't worth my time." Who are we kidding, they think that after ten times. Women know it's worth their time. Changing that diaper is not about what they're doing in that moment; they know it's about what they're building for the future. For women, it's easier to appreciate gratification that comes later, whereas men often want instant gratification.

Women also are known for their intuition. We have a gut check when we make decisions—decisions like buying houses, for instance. We go with our gut. It almost always works out to be the best choice.

As women, we walk into a house and we know there's going to be a family living there, so it's natural for us to put ourselves into the mind and the shoes of the potential buyers. I'm not sure that men think as much about the people that are going to be living there, as they do about the man cave and garage space. Ok, maybe that's not fair, because I know a lot of amazing guy flippers, but my sense is that it's a bit more top of mind for women that there will be a family living there, so they ask if it makes sense to have a kitchen set up a certain way, or have so many bathrooms or bedrooms. We ask ourselves, "Is the house functional and fixed up? Will it turn into a home as well as turn a profit?"

Given our innate ability to trust our instincts and use our intuition, when it comes to making sound real estate investment choices, women could very well have the upper hand. Don't let anyone tell you otherwise. Regardless of our fun banter and girl-power attitude, it doesn't matter whether men or women are better at investing. The point is, you as a woman can invest safely and wisely. Learn to trust yourself; your inner guidance will never let you down.

B. Taking Responsibility - Reality Check

Let's start by asking, how can you do more with less? Begin to look at all the alternate ways you can have the same quality of life and the same experiences, all while saving money. This skill will come in very handy when you are flipping homes. Imagine somebody gave each of us $1,000 to spend this week. If we knew that somebody was going to look at it, even just ourselves, at the end of the week and say, "Here's what I did with my $1,000," what would it reveal? There's a story in the Bible, Matthew 25:14-30, about a master who goes away on a trip. Before he goes, he entrusts two bags of gold to his top servant, two bags of silver to his next best servant, and one bag of silver to his laziest worker. The top servant wisely invests the two bags of gold, and earns another two bags while the master is gone. The next best servant did the same thing, investing the silver and earning two more bags. The lazy worker buried the money in the ground, in an attempt to ensure the money was not lost. Of course, when the master returned, he was delighted by the first two servants and how they had grown his money, and he banished the lazy worker for not having done anything to grow his money. The point is, sticking it in a hole is dumb. Squandering it is dumb. The only respectable thing is to grow money that's entrusted to you.

I have an example from my own life. My son was born in 2004; I was supposed to return to my job from maternity leave on a Monday. The Friday before, I got a call that the company I was working for was merging with another company. I lost my job, and got a severance package. Instead of using it to buy the latest, fanciest baby gear...I used it to buy my first investment property.

Let's take a look at how Tara, Cathy and Rebecca would spend $1,000. They'll each explain how they once would have spent it, and how they see themselves spending it now.

Teacher Tara

$1,000! If I got handed $1,000 a few years ago, I would have put it directly into my bank—into my emergency savings account, to be exact, an account I have never had to access but one which always has a year of my wages ready, without fail.

Of course, now if I were handed $1,000, I think I would spend it a little differently. I would put it into the new business account I have, and save it toward purchasing an investment property. So maybe I haven't changed that much? I'd still save the money, but I'd buy a home sooner than I'll (hopefully) ever need to spend my emergency fund.

Corporate Cathy

$1,000! If someone gave me $1,000 a few years ago it would have been gone within the day—to groceries, swimming lessons, new runners for the kids, Starbucks, and taking the family out for dinner. Money came in and went out quite fluidly, back in my corporate days, pre-divorce. I spent it willingly and I always thought it was stuff we couldn't live without.

Now, with $1,000, I would spend it on more education. Working with Maggie has only revealed the tip of the iceberg. I might take an online course, or a two-day seminar, or purchase a few books. Of course, this is after I take out half and put it in my new investment savings account.

Retired Rebecca

$1,000! What a windfall! A few years ago I would have spent it on donations to charities, gifts for my family, buying food to feed everyone when they came home for Thanksgiving, and then buying extra so we could run leftovers down to the food bank.

Now? I suppose now it will go under the mattress — what I call our retirement fund. My husband and I have made it a priority to get our finances together, and I think saving that $1,000 to go toward eventually purchasing an investment property will be the best use of it for us. After attending the seminar, my first goal has been to find us a small cash-flowing rental.

Tara, Cathy, and Rebecca are on the upward trajectory of managing their money. If we looked at a less money-savvy, modern-day woman given $1,000, she might spend it on lunch with her girlfriends, or to buy a new purse or have Starbucks every day.

I actually used to go to the movies once a week with my kids. If we went on "Movie Tuesdays," the movies were only $5 and they had free popcorn. Now, we won't go to the movies any other day besides Movie Tuesdays. Before you call me cheap, hear me out.

Getting movie tickets and buying popcorn on a regular day is at least $80 for my husband and I and four of my kids. On Movie Tuesdays, it's only $30. This means that for less than half-price we have the same exact experience. This is a good example of how we can do things just slightly differently and build wealth, while not suffering or sacrificing our experiences. Now I can take that extra $50 and invest it, either into an account to save for a property, or in another activity that will improve my lifestyle. That's the way I'm always thinking about things.

Another significant way I've cut expenses is by using a bookkeeper from India. He charges me $36 a week. Before I hired him, I was paying a part-time bookkeeper in the United States as much as $250 a week, and they weren't nearly as good as my $36 per week guy.

I know people who always park valet. It's an additional $5 to valet park rather than self-park. For them, it's worth it not to have to deal with parking and to have someone else take care of the car. What I want to know is what else could they be doing with that $5 that's smarter? It adds up, just like that Starbucks habit. Park waaaay in the back of the lot where there are open spaces and… save $5 on valet parking and burn an additional five calories by walking the extra distance! Imagine if we're going to the movies every single week, spending $80 for six of us, versus going only on Tuesdays, paying $30? Over the course of a year, that's a savings of $2,600, just for going to the movies on a different day. Same movie, same theatre, same popcorn… just a different day. How smart does that feel? Now if we only went once a month, sacrificing a small amount of lifestyle, but certainly still enjoying a little entertainment, we would be saving an additional $1,200.

Here's a quick story. I was at one of my property sites that had just wrapped up construction. There were a

> **SUPER FRUGAL**
> $360/year for 1x/month
> on Movie Tuesday
>
> **SUPER SMART**
> $1,560/year for 1x/week
> on Movie Tuesday
>
> **STUPID**
> $960/year for 1x/month
> for Regular Priced Movie Day
>
> **SUPER STUPID**
> $4,160/year for 1x/week
> for Regular Priced Movie Day

few leftover bags of Quikrete—some inexpensive building materials. I said to my contractors, "You're going to return that for store credit, right?" They gave me this strange look and said, "It's just Quikrete." I picked the bags up myself, threw them in the back of my car, drove straight to the Home Depot and got my $16 store credit. I understood, but my contractors did not, that wealth is built, or squandered, $5 and $10 and $20 at a time.

Having a car is also a great example. How often do you need a new car? How many miles do you put on your car before you think it's time to get a new one? Did your best friend get a new car and all of a sudden you have a new car? Can you afford the car you currently drive?

Even the smallest daily behavior can be an opportunity to save money. Look at how much food you throw away at the end of the week. We know some of our

(margin note) Wealth is built $5 at a time.

FlipChick sisters that excel at meal planning – they plan out the groceries for the week, and in the planning, they save money. There is a survey by VISA that found that the average person spends $11 when they go out to lunch. That's $55 a week, more than $2,500 a year, versus people who bring their lunch to work who spend $6.38 a day. It's exactly those numbers. Take the $11 and whatever cents, and $6 and whatever cents. You can use a compounding calculator. Let's say once a year you invest $2,500 and you add 12% interest, which is very conservative if you're talking about a real estate return, and look at the $6 invested versus the $11 invested. It's the same thing. You'll see the compounding—how much faster the other one grows.

In the afternoon of Day One of her three-day seminar, Rebecca was invited to consider her spending in much the same vein. Let's see what she came up with.

Retired Rebecca

I had finally recognized that all our coffees out and dinners out were adding up. Before the morning session was through that day, I was frantically trying to tally up what my husband and I spent money on each week, and what areas we could cut.

I spent my lunch break doing this exercise and it was a real eye-opener. I saw that even if I bought lunch only one of my work days, I was still spending nearly $20 a week, because I was buying food from airports. Whenever I was late or in a rush, I bought my lunch. Those days occurred more often than not. I had to be brutally honest: When I added it up and considered averages, I found I was spending $67 a week on eating out! I then added it up for my husband, who often wrote off his

EXERCISE: TRACK YOUR EXPENSES FOR ONE WEEK

Tracking your expenses alone will probably shave 20-25% off of where you're spending money. It's the awareness that you're spending $500 a month at Starbucks. Become deliberate about your spending.

At the end of the week, list three things where you have been spending more money than you realized, or spending money without intent.
EX: Meals out, lattes, etc.

Now brainstorm and list a few alternate ways you can have the same quality of life and the same experiences, without spending as much money. Refer to our examples above.

business lunches. He easily spent $150 on lunches in a week when he was entertaining clients.

I looked at what we spent on groceries. I realized why I was always throwing food away. I wondered why I never just brought my lunch – especially knowing that airport food is pricey and unhealthy. I felt a bit ashamed, really, looking at this part of my life under a microscope. I was too lazy to prepare my lunch. That was the only reason. I was hopeful that seeing a new way of managing and investing my money would motivate me to find any extra money I had, so I could start playing with this new ideology I was learning.

The Power of Asking Questions

Questions are curative because they change your focus. If you ever feel frustrated as you are going through this process of owning your life, your wealth, and your relationships, ask yourself questions to identify the source of that frustration. And don't just identify it, but see the value of that frustration. Dr. Carol Carnes says that frustration – or that sense of "I can't do this anymore" – indicates that something else is wanting to emerge through you. And it indicates there's something else *there* to emerge. You wouldn't be frustrated if that's the only reality you could have. Your heart knows that that which is trying to emerge is trying to tell you something. Don't interpret frustration as "failure" on your part; interpret it as a message from your soul: there's more and you ought to have it.

Frustration will help you move forward as a driving force that goes towards the pleasure and away from pain. In order to improve our lives and ourselves, we need some element of pain. If something is not painful enough, we are not going to improve. If a relationship is mediocre, what's the motivation for it? If nobody is slamming doors and making smoke detectors fall off the ceiling, how will we know what to fix?

Pain motivates. We just have to push past all the stories in our head about why something is not going to work or why it's going to be too hard—these are stories based on mostly nothing, and they have to go. But first you must raise your level of awareness. If you aren't even aware of the root cause that your pain stems from, you'll expend all of your energy dwelling on the symptoms, rather than the issues that hold the secrets to your own genuine growth. Make a special note here that your root cause often sits behind the blame and the hurt you've assumed are being caused by someone else.

All the roadblocks, the stuff that shows up that keeps us from moving on will only ever shift when we take full responsibility for our own lives and results. If you blame others for your problems, you put the power in their hands to keep you down. This is good news, because with this simple new awareness we can all take control of our own lives immediately – discarding old stories about how for us to be successful we need someone else to change. If you're running from pain, you're missing the big lessons. Try sitting in it for a bit – and see what it has to teach you. Pain is always the instigator for changing ourselves, our identities and how we choose to show up in the world.

So how do you apply this lesson? For example, if you have a headache, don't just take an aspirin. Ask a question. Let the headache be a sign to you of some cause that needs to change. Did you not get enough sleep, or not drink enough water? Things don't happen spontaneously. There is a cause and effect.

Frustration, like a headache, is symptomatic of something you either did or didn't do. So ask yourself questions!

To OWN IT! means you are taking responsibility for it. And by "responsibility," we do not mean blame, fault or guilt. We want to be empowered and freed up by it, we want to stop the lying and pretending. You want to be in control and not controlled by your finances.

We have a funny relationship with control. The definition of control is: the power to influence or direct people's behavior or the course of events. And this is what we want you to have control over - your wealth, your life, your relationships. Think how much power and freedom you have from being able to influence or direct your own behavior or the course of events. If you have the power to influence your finances, then you have freedom.

C. Replace Your Income

A good first wealth milestone is to replace your income with passive income. You can begin by developing a strategy that covers your expenses. Maggie took Cathy through such a strategy. Let's see how it worked for her.

Corporate Cathy

Throughout my sessions with Maggie we worked a lot with my money stuff. I've been carrying about $20,000 worth of debt at any given time for the past decade, so of course Maggie lasered in on that and worked with me to come up with a plan to eliminate it – fast. That seemed pretty basic. It was the strategy she offered next that really changed things for me.

Maggie kept telling me to replace my income. I was making $120,000 a year, so I couldn't imagine what else I could do to replace my income. One day, during an in-person session at a downtown bistro, she scratched out a map on a napkin as to how I could replace my income. It was this funny little note, almost indecipherable, but I kept it.

She suggested that I consider buying a house solely to flip. Based on her drawing and experience, she figured I could make $25,000 from flipping a home. Then, three months later, I would do it again. By the end of the conversation, Maggie had given me a five-year road map to replacing my income. She had me thinking I could flip one house per quarter, and invest the profit into a rental. This way, if I wanted to replace $120,000, I wanted a $10,000 a month rental income, so I needed twenty rental properties each netting $500 per month. With $25,000 per quarter coming in from the flipped homes, for every quarter I could be adding another rental property. Within just twenty quarters, I could replace my income.

I was blown away. Elated. I felt light as air after that conversation. Sure, I didn't have any property yet, or even know where I would buy something, but Maggie had shown me a formula that could lift me out of the stuck-ness and into a world where my bucket list was actually achievable. I just had to take the first step. With Maggie's guidance, taking that first step was easy – and fun.

Three Types of Income

Wealthy people measure their wealth in terms of net worth. They don't say, "How much money do you make a year?" They talk about net worth. How much you made for this year doesn't matter. Is your net worth increasing? If you were worth $5 million last year, are you worth $6 million this year or $4 million? It doesn't matter if you made $1 million this year. If your net worth went down, it's a loss.

Wealthy people also measure their wealth in terms of their passive income, also known as their investment income. Are you making money regardless of whether you are doing something or not doing something?

Rebecca decided she and her husband needed to have a heart-to-heart about net worth. She was surprised by how well the conversation went.

Retired Rebecca

"Honey, let's have a conversation." I said out of the blue one Sunday morning. It was a week after I had finished my seminar. We were sitting at the kitchen table, reading the weekend newspaper with our coffee. I had been thinking about this topic all week, and I knew we needed to discuss it.

"Sure, what about?" my husband said amiably.

"Oh, our net worth." I laughed. "If we know what that is, for starters."

My husband laughed with me. "I think I have an idea."

We had our first frank and open discussion about money since we were in our twenties. We had both just fallen so deeply into our routine of life together, that we had never taken the time to really assess the state of our finances. Apart from when we wrote our wills together when the kids were little, it was a non-issue.

It felt good to have this conversation and to evaluate not only where we were financially but to see where we were in the context of our friends. It's not like we talk about money with our friends, but as my husband is in a few men's business groups he had done his fair share of gossiping, and he seemed to have a sense of where other people were at.

What we both agreed upon was that we needed to shift our investment strategies and look into some new options. We wanted to update our current portfolio, and we were both excited about my new education in real estate investing.

As the conversation wore on, we both became excited about our future. We saw how we could create a plan to generate the income we wanted to retire with. And as we chatted and daydreamed that Sunday morning together, there was no holding us back. It felt like we were in our twenties again, both of us optimistic and hopeful.

There are three types of income: residual income, passive income and active income. What we're doing right now when we rehab and rent is a form of gaining a "residual income." We show up, we do the work of fixing up the house, and for the rest of our ownership of that house, we are paid residually. We did the work up front and reap the benefits as long as we keep the property. Remember again the story of the golden goose? Our rental portfolio is our golden goose.

"Passive income" is like the apartment building that I just bought. I showed up at a closing, I signed some paperwork, I drove to the apartment building one time, and every month I get paid $5,000. That's real investing. I even have a property manager who manages it. I actually have very little involvement in the day-to-day operations of my passive income.

The goal, really, is to be managing your money. Because that's your job after all, to manage your money. We talk about what we will do when we no longer want to flip houses, and we are excited to move into different ways of managing our money. That's its own skillset; looking at your assets and seeing what assets are depreciating, what's worth what, and which ones you want to hold on to.

"Active income" is when you show up and get paid for adding value one time. This is also known as trading hours for dollars. Flipping houses is active income, even if you're not doing the physical work yourself, you get one payout one time. It's a great source of active income, but it's still income you cash out on once.

So again to recap, when we flip a house it's active income, we get the profit and that's it. If we buy a house, fix it up and rent it out, that's residual income. If we just buy an already turn-key property, that's the act of a true investor. That's the goal; you get to a place where you just show up, write the check once and get paid an infinite number of times.

It's time to decide: What are you going to do with your money? Most people aren't willing to give up their gratification now for their long-term future, and that's what sets a FlipChick apart from most people.

D. Compounding - Start Now, Finish Rich

Do you know what the "secret sauce" is to your real estate flipping business? That one ingredient that differentiates you as a FlipChick business woman from a casual hobbyist flipper? If there's one takeaway from this book that we want you to remember, it's the importance of COMPOUNDING: The concept of reinvesting profit from one property to turn additional profit from another property (without investing any new capital!) – and doing it again, and again, and again.

> "Compound interest is the eighth wonder of the world. He who understands it, earns it... he who doesn't... pays it."
> **– Albert Einstein**

Compounding is such a critical concept to your success as a FlipChick that I want to make sure you fully understand it. Did you know that compounding is happening in your life right now? You might not recognize it as compounding, but if you look at every piece of evidence in your life, whether it's the size pants you wear or the amount of money in your bank account, it is a result of the choices you've made. There are certain choices that, over time, have compounded to create your exact circumstances.

For example, what food you choose to eat every day, what activities you participate in, what books you choose to read. You're getting more of whatever it is that you're consuming, and when you're consuming the same thing every day, it's going to keep compounding.

We want to teach you to appreciate the value of compounding through a demonstration. Let's look at health. We have two choices. We can get up in the morning and have an Egg McMuffin, or we can get up in the morning and have a smoothie or a handful of nuts and an apple.

Let's say that my neighbor and I each have a different routine. Her routine is to get up and go to McDonald's in the morning on the way to work, and have an Egg McMuffin, starting day one. So we're at day one of compounding this effect. I am starting too, but instead I have a handful of nuts and an apple at the same time every morning.

After a week, there might be zero difference. We look the same, she may feel more fulfilled because her food comes from the drive-through, and it tastes yummy. After a month, there is still really no difference. She might be one pound heavier than me. But compound it and fast-forward it, and then over whatever period of time, say, six months, by then she'll be ten pounds heavier and I will actually be five pounds lighter. In day one, you don't notice it. In day two, you don't notice it. In week one, you don't notice it. In month one, you might notice it.

Let's talk about compounding in real estate to acquire rental properties. To illustrate an example, let's first make the assumption that you're flipping four houses per year—you start with one house per quarter. Let's also assume that you're profiting $25,000 from each of the flips. Assumption number three is that you're investing that $25,000 each quarter by using it to buy a rental unit. In other words, you're banking your flipping capital—you're not spending it. You're not out buying a boat, buying a car, or buying anything else that isn't going to build your business. Being a successful investor requires having the discipline to know that your long-term goal is more important than that fancy car.

Now, let's make another assumption that your net rental income is $500 per month. This is where some really cool stuff starts to happen. Every quarter, you're giving yourself a $500 a month raise, which each new rental property that you buy. It's like Monopoly—every time you pass Go, you collect your money. Every time you take action and follow these steps, you receive a $500 a month raise every quarter. You're adding a property to your investment portfolio. You're growing your empire.

Let's take a look at a six-year projection. In year one, you're buying one property per quarter. By year two, you're getting one "free" rental property bought from your rental income. Year three, you're getting two rental properties paid for with your rental income. At year four, you start to see the compounding effect happen—I call this the "buy one get one free" stage. You end up at a place where you're starting to see three "free" properties in a quarter, while doing no additional work. You go from one rental property for free, to nine properties for free in year six. Every single year, you're getting more rental properties from the income from your rentals than you were from your flipping income.

Now, let's look at the annual income from all rental properties. The first year, you'd be getting $24,000. The next year, $54,000. The third year, $84,000. By the fourth year, you're making a six-figure income—not just from flipping, but from rental income—without needing to work. If you're frugal, you won't need to spend

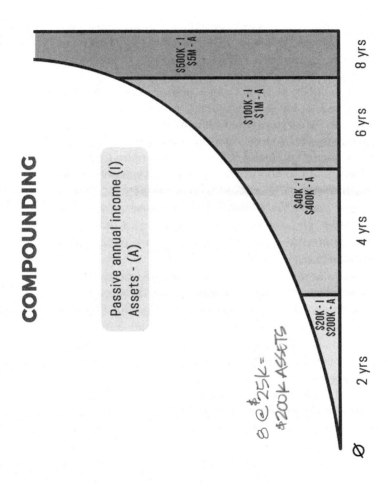

all of that money. If your happy point is $75,000 or $80,000 per year, you can put the rest in the bank and build a portfolio of assets to leave for those you love and care about. Or, you can continue compounding—even just two years later you will have doubled your amount of passive income. It just keeps growing, as long as you stay on this track.

Remember, wealthy people measure their wealth in terms of net worth, not how much money they "make" per year. So let's take a look at your asset value using this technique. The first year, your assets are worth $100,000. The second year, they're worth $225,000. Following through, $350,000 in the third year, $500,000 in the fourth year. At that point, you've added $100,000 of assets simply by reinvesting your rental income. By year five, your assets are at $675,000, and in year six $825,000. By year seven, you have a portfolio of over a million dollars!

Since no equity was added to that number, one million dollars is a very conservative number. Since it's assumed you're buying properties that are under market value, even with your rental properties, it's very reasonable to say that that number is closer to 1.5 million dollars or even 2 million dollars depending on where you're buying and what you're buying.

And remember, real estate properties always appreciate over any five to ten-year period. When you go past five or ten years, or if you're in a really dynamic market, you could be on the higher end of that appreciation. You could therefore double the asset values we have laid out here.

These aren't just hypothetical projections. This can be your reality. So ask yourself, what goal works for you?

EXERCISE: REFLECTION - COMPOUNDING LIFE RESULTS

Identify the results that you are seeing to the actions you have been taking in the past that are compounding these results. If you weigh 200 pounds and you want to weigh 150 pounds, identify what has been compounding to get you to 200 pounds and identify what you need to do to get to 150 pounds. Ask yourself:

What have I done that has gotten me here?

What would I need to do to have $10,000 in my bank account, or $100,000 in my bank account?

RESULTS [Ex: I weigh 200 lbs.]

PAST ACTIONS [Ex: Exercise once a week]

NEW ACTIONS TO TAKE [Ex: Exercise 3x a week, hire a trainer]

What are you going after? It's different for everybody. I know that for my family, our number for what we consider to be a high quality of life is higher than $100,000 annual income. So what would make *your* life amazing? Do you want to take this compounding strategy out to ten years for yourself? What would you like your annual income to be? What do you want your legacy to be? There's no judgment, no right or wrong.

Hopefully, you understand how simple it is to use compounding to increase your wealth. But remember—in the beginning, it's painfully slow. It's like eating that cheeseburger every day, you're not going to see it show up for a little while... then BAM heart attack. Both simple and compound interest START OUT at the same place. The compounding is stacking the result. My neighbor didn't start out eating ten Egg McMuffins, she started out with one. I started out with one apple and a handful of almonds. And we could not notice an immediate difference at first.

You don't have to work smarter or work harder, you just have to take the same action, over and over again. This is the nature of compounding. You are exactly where you are based on the decisions you have made and the belief structures that underlie those decisions. If you want to change your circumstances, then you have to look at those decisions and beliefs and understand them. If you don't understand them, you're going to have to be able to change them.

Be kind and forgiving to yourself throughout this process. The consistent choices you make each day are what is compounding in your life. Recognize that when you go backwards, it doesn't mean that you have to stay there. Forgive yourself for the blips in the road.

Wealth Isn't an Accident

Surprise! There is no such thing as getting rich quick. Don't be duped. Well, okay, you might be able to get "rich" quick, but you certainly can't get wealthy quick. Wealth is inherently built on a strong foundation of principles. There are plenty of basketball players and actors who may be rich, but certainly aren't wealthy. People who don't have money

> "It's easy to get rich....
> I want you to get and
> stay wealthy."
> – **Margaret Wright**

tend to have this misconception of people with money and how they got it. It's the must-be-nice mentality. Like somehow the money just showed up for these rich people. Somehow they woke up and they had a yacht, or a million dollars in the bank.

Your bank account might make it appear that you're rich, but wealth is built on a foundation of strength and structure. You can get rich, but you want to stay wealthy.

It blows my mind when I see how many people can make a million dollars in a year, or in five years, and then it vanishes. It's so common. I see people who made $25,000 one year, the next year they made $50,000, the next year $75,000, the next year $100,000 and they still have nothing. If you were living on $25,000, then when you were making $100,000 you could have socked away $75,000 by living well below your means, but not below a lifestyle you previously lived. Living beyond your means is the true distinguisher between rich and wealthy. Wealthy people don't live beyond their means.

How many sports players have you read or heard about who just get too old and then they have nothing left? Or celebrities who have gone bankrupt? True wealth is not about getting rich; it's about knowing how to use the money you have so that it works for you, so you don't have to work for your money. True wealth is about learning how to manage money, not just how to acquire it. Truly wealthy people don't squander a cent; they love their money, value it, treat it with respect, and have a healthy relationship to it. When you look at wealth this way, you see that it really has nothing to do with the money at all – and everything to do with all that stuff we talked about in the earlier sections. How you do anything is how you do everything. So how do you grow and keep your wealth? This is the most powerful lesson you can learn.

If you study wealthy people, you observe that they have certain traits. There is a great book, *The Millionaire Next Door*, that talks about what wealthy people spend their money on and it's not what most people think. The average millionaire drives a seven-year old car that they bought used and paid cash for. They don't own a watch that costs over $100. They don't have a mortgage. What wealthy people spend their money on is different than what middle-class people spend their money on, and it is the opposite of what the middle class would expect.

Being a good steward of the money you have is one more way you can make a difference in the world. It's time to redefine money, wealth, and all your associations with it, and to repurpose your relationship with money so that it leaves a legacy of good, not just a closet of dusty shoes. Let's take a look at how Tara, Cathy and

Rebecca progressed on their journey for financial independence.

Teacher Tara

After my course was done, I took the plunge and explored my first investment. I rented a small apartment and sublet it at a daily rate that was five times what I was paying for rent. I enjoyed decorating it so much, and I loved putting in all these nice little touches to make people feel at home. In no time, I was booked daily and I collected enough money to pay the rent in the first week of the month. Every month, I saved the rest to put towards another property. I'm looking at buying my first home within the next two months.

In addition to investing my money in a way that will allow it to grow, the self-discovery work that I did throughout the whole process has helped me the most. Once I took control of my money in a new way, I was also able to take stock and see how lucky I was. I had a job I loved, that I never wanted to leave. I had financial security. Maybe it was time to find that husband after all.

As fate would have it, I met my future husband when he came to rent my apartment. He was working remotely and he stayed for a week. When he arrived, we had an instant attraction. Before the week was through, he had invited me for dinner and we made a connection. We began seeing each other that week, and the rest is history. Tonight, he will be on my arm as we attend a benefit. It is amazing to me how changing my life and behavior in one aspect actually changed my life in all aspects.

Corporate Cathy

Within three months of working with Maggie, I felt like a new woman. I began having so much more free time. I stopped doing all the things I didn't like doing. I no longer had to do laundry and run the kids around. I have felt a sense of freedom in my life that I hadn't felt in a really long time.

As I recently prepared to go to a benefit for Peruvian young moms and their babies, I looked at myself in the mirror. I saw that I was smiling, just smiling. I didn't have anything particularly exciting happening in my life in that moment to smile about, but there I was, smiling. I had not felt that in control of my life in a long time. The benefit was for a great cause, and there I was, an active, involved participant in it. I was no longer a stuck woman who couldn't stand being in her cubicle one more minute. I was on my way to financial freedom, and nothing could stop me.

Retired Rebecca

After that seminar, my life changed completely. With-in a few months, my husband and I decided to get a kick start on retirement and take a vacation to Peru. I wanted to try something different, so we went there to volunteer at an orphanage for part of the trip.

By the time we went to Peru, I had already begun my investing adventure. I was feeling confident – and I knew that I was on the right track. The seminar had only kick-started the process. The people I met, and the opportunities that presented themselves in the wake of that seminar fell into my lap effortlessly.

At the all-girls orphanage in Peru, I noticed that no-body was stepping up to help those girls. Lots of volunteers would show up, people with time – like college kids, gap-year kids, people who have time but not much money. They could show up and change diapers, but if there was no money for diapers, somebody with money had to show up and provide it for the girls.

I saw that there were only so many resources available, resources that came through an exchange that was not tied to money. I felt frustrated seeing this. People would show up and want to make a difference, and their help was often turned away because they needed money more than people and time. The orphanage needed to pay the rent, the salaries of staff and tutors. What I saw was that without the financial support, the people making a difference on the ground could only do so much, and for me... it wasn't enough.

I got to know some of the older girls in the orphanage and learned that resources were in place to take care of their basic physical needs, but they were not able to go to school. They were not getting any education, or even life-skills training. Some of the girls even had babies, victims of rape. Many of the girls had been abused. They were doing the best they could to care for the younger girls in the orphanage.

I got pretty close to two of the young moms at the orphanage. It broke my heart that these young moms were trying their best to be good moms, but their fate was likely that when they turned eighteen, they would end up on the streets, and their babies would be taken away to another orphanage, because they didn't have the education or resources to find the means to care for their children. I didn't know what to do, but I knew I had to do something. With some of the other volunteers, I talked about the possibility of foster care, or finding someone to adopt them. I had no idea what I could do, but decided then and there that this was my calling.

What did something different look like? It took money. I was so motivated to create passive income that within a month I found a small apartment building and with the income from the apartment building, I was able to pay the rent for a small complex in Peru, and we opened a home for young mothers who were victims of abuse. It's a huge financial commitment to support what has grown to house twenty moms and babies now, but to give these beautiful souls a safe home, an education and hope for a future they never dreamt of… it is priceless.

Tonight's benefit is to raise money to expand the program and transition the program to be under a group of local nuns. I've been organizing this benefit for months and I feel ready to make this transition. The best part is, this year of creating the home has kept me busy, and allowed my husband time to wrap up and transition his own business. Now, after tonight's benefit, we are both going to be fully retired. Not only that, but we have a stash of money ready for us to retire with. It didn't take long once I shifted my mindset and changed some habits.

I think the most effective lesson I took away from the seminar I went to, the one that really started me on this journey, was just that I could do it. That things can change, and be done differently. I realized that I didn't have to think or do the same things over and over again. I could try new things. There were so many ideas, resources, and opportunities available. The seminar facilitators were so inspiring and optimistic. Women in the seminar alongside me beamed and emerged refreshed and fully charged with new and exciting ideas. I think it was the inspiration and hope we all felt that day that led us all to start making changes.

When I did start to make changes, way back at the early stage, my time was what I really had to control. I kicked some big time-wasting habits I had – like watching *Live! With Kelly and Michael* with my coffee every morning – and began learning about real estate in every little bit of free time I had. Changing up my coffee and TV routine allowed me to get an even earlier start on my day, and within a month I didn't miss it. In fact, I couldn't believe I wasn't starting my day until 10 a.m. every time I watched TV with my coffee. It felt so wasteful.

Making that one small change allowed me to get up and out earlier in Peru, too. Which led us to the orphanage, to volunteering, to all of the excitement of this evening. It's funny, how one simple change, a simple habit I thought nothing of, could bring so much goodness into my life.

Sharing Wealth with the World

Tara arrived early and settled in with her boyfriend. Rebecca was busy working at the registration table, greeting the guests and handing out goodie bags made up of kindly donated items, some of which were from Peruvian sponsors. People were paying a lot to be here and support the cause, and Rebecca felt so grateful that she wanted to ensure the guests had a premier experience.

As Tara and her boyfriend sipped wine at the table, Cathy arrived. She approached Tara's table and asked if she could join them.

"Of course!" Tara beamed, genuinely welcoming. With her new beau and new confidence, Tara felt more outgoing.

As Cathy and Tara started chatting, they realized they had a lot in common. Cathy shared about her coach, and how she was beginning to invest in real estate.

"Me too!" Tara exclaimed. Then Tara proceeded to tell Cathy about the course she had taken, and how much it had taught her. She shared about her vacation rental success, and the excitement and potential she felt around her first flip house.

Cathy was intrigued about the course, and made a note in her phone to look it up.

"You won't be sorry," Tara said. "It was the best investment I could have ever made."

Later in the evening, Rebecca milled around as the guests enjoyed their dinner. She stopped at Tara and Cathy's table. Cathy smiled at Rebecca and waved her over.

"Rebecca, right?" Cathy asked. Rebecca nodded and smiled.

"I just want to say congratulations on a wonderful benefit. It is really a great thing, what you're doing. You've certainly inspired us!" Tara nodded at Cathy's words.

Rebecca smiled at the ladies. "Thank you so much. Would you believe it was a seminar I took in real estate investing, of all things, that was the first step in this crazy journey?" She laughed. Tara gasped in recognition and Cathy laughed.

"Oh my goodness," Tara said, "That's exactly what we have in common here, too! I took a course, Cathy worked with a coach. It's changed our lives!"

"Hasn't it?" Rebecca laughed. "Looks like we're in the sisterhood. Can I have your cards? This is too much of a coincidence. Let's get together. We can share our tips."

Cathy and Tara nodded and handed Rebecca their cards. The ladies clinked their wine glasses. "To real estate!" they all exclaimed, before taking a sip.

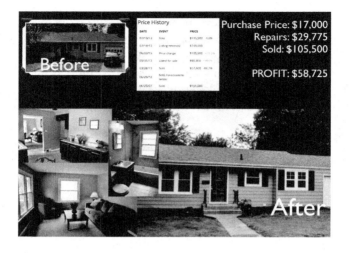

CONCLUSION

Tara, Cathy, and Rebecca are composites of real women—FlipChicks—who our sisterhood has helped in their quest to succeed as real estate investors, and in life. If it's possible for them, believe me— it's possible for you.

For best results, you need to attend to all of the things in this book before you ever even consider your first home. Don't gloss over the importance of any of these elements. It may not seem like hiring someone to take tasks off your plate or that cleaning up your mindset and your language is important, but if you do not place a high value on these life areas, you run the risk of continuing to have what you have always had. Don't be fooled. And take action! It's better to make progress in a disastrous way than to be stagnant.

This book was intended to have you begin to ask questions and look at the areas of your life that aren't working. Now that you know what's possible, what are you going to do about it? If you've made it to the end of this book, then perhaps you have begun to seriously consider flipping homes as your primary source of income (either part time or full time) to create a secure future for yourself and your family... just like I have.

My Gift to You

So how can you get started investing in real estate? I have a training I want to gift to all of you who have read this book and want to create your own wealth in real estate by flipping homes. The best part is, I am going to give it to you for free.

What's the catch? There is no catch. This is my WHY: It's my vision to build a community of thousands of FlipChicks around the country who are successfully flipping homes… a FlipChick sisterhood. The faster this training gets into the hands of women who want to replace their income flipping homes, the faster we build our community. It's that simple.

The course is called, "How to Find and Flip Your First Home in 91 Days," and it will show you how to start and build a real estate business flipping homes in your own back yard.

You will learn:

- The exact how-to steps to start flipping homes, even if you aren't the least bit handy
- How to successfully flip your first home in just 91 days
- How to avoid the costly mistakes most women home-flippers make (especially on their first two projects)
- How to know if the home you want to flip is going to make you a lot of money or be a total flop
- How to turn flipping homes into a full-time or part-time business so you can replace your income, divorce your day job, and spend more time with your family… because you will no longer be trading hours of your time for a paycheck

You can access this free training at www.flipchick-coaching.com/webinar.

Welcome to the FlipChick sisterhood!

ACKNOWLEDGEMENTS

My heart is overflowing with gratitude for so many beautiful souls whose paths have crossed mine in the making of this book. To my babies, all growing up too fast, you have been the inspiration for everything great I have done—all of which pale in comparison to how proud I am of each of you. Tyler, Braedyn, Nathan, Anika, Finn and Noah. I love you more than life.

To the love of my life, Nate, you showed me true passion in love, in life, in all we do. You are my best friend. Above all, you taught me it wouldn't be easy, but definitely worth it.

To my editor, Karen, you are masterful at getting into my brain and picking out the best parts to put on paper, and surprise, it didn't even hurt…that much.

ABOUT THE AUTHOR

Margaret Wright is a powerhouse in business and an expert at flipping houses. Born and raised in Chicago, she is a best-selling author & speaker, philanthropist, business owner & one of the most sought-after Real Estate Investment Consultants in the country.

A former computer scientist, she quickly tired of working in the corporate IT industry, and started and ran several businesses before founding FlipChick Coaching. Margaret was not an overnight sensation. She was a teen mom, turned computer geek, turned business owner, turned real estate success story, but she was always an entrepreneur at heart. Having made millions in real estate, and with more than 100 flips and hundreds of transactions under her belt, Margaret wanted to help women take back their financial independence. Beyond helping others build passive income, Margaret teaches the principles of building solid real estate investment portfolios. By developing a simple and easy to understand system, laser focused on building generational wealth, Margaret has helped thousands of people learn how to "Divorce Their Day Job" and never live paycheck to paycheck again.

Passionate about inspiring women to believe in themselves, and get their dreams off the shelf so they can become reality, Margaret herself loves living a lifestyle of her creation, which includes travel, quality time with their children, and dreaming up new business ideas with her husband, Nate.

APPENDIX

You may be a real estate investor if...

1. You spend more time on Zillow than Facebook.
2. When you reach into your purse to grab your wallet, you pull out a measuring tape instead.
3. Your high heels are covered in mud.
4. You are on a first-name basis with the guys at Home Depot.
5. You have an electrician, a plumber and an HVAC guy on speed dial.
6. An ideal first date is driving around looking at vacant properties.
7. You have seen every episode of Rehab Addict and have no idea who the Kardashians are.
8. Your favorite accessory is a hard hat.
9. The only paint on your nails comes from your contractor's brush. /Your nicely manicured hands are always covered in exterior paint.
10. You make more money than your man. And he thinks it's hot.

NOTES

NOTES

NOTES

NOTES

NOTES

NOTES

NOTES

NOTES

CPSIA information can be obtained
at www.ICGtesting.com
Printed in the USA
FSOW03n0357070417
32769FS